Quilt as Desired

Charlene C. Frable

©2007 Charlene C. Frable
Published by

krause publications
An Imprint of F+W Publications

**700 East State Street • Iola, WI 54990-0001
715-445-2214 • 888-457-2873
www.krausebooks.com**

Our toll-free number to place an order or obtain
a free catalog is (800) 258-0929.

The following registered trademark terms and companies appear in this publication:
Pfaff, Baby Lock, Quilter's Choice Professional, Free-Motion Slider, Sulky, Golden Threads,
Schmetz, Madeira, Collins, Quilter's Choice, IDT, Omnigrid, Kwik Klip, YLI, Mettler

Library of Congress Catalog Number: 2006935548

ISBN-13: 978-0-89689-479-2

Edited by Andy Belmas
Designed by Heidi Bittner-Zastrow

Printed in China

Acknowledgments

I would like to thank the following individuals for helping to turn my dream into a reality:

My husband, Barry, who supports my every endeavor.

My parents, Bill and Sally Coleman, who encouraged me to pursue my passions in life.

To my sister, Phyllis Coleman Post, who took me to my first quilt show. Phyllis also pieced one of the quilts used in Section One.

To Diana Slopik, who steered my passion for quilting towards teaching.

To every quilter I have met through my classes. Your questions and your zeal to finish your own quilts have made me a better teacher. For that, I am grateful.

Baby Lock USA for the use of the Baby Lock Quilter's Choice Professional sewing machine for the photo shoot.

Pat LaPierre for her encouragement and LaPierre Studio for the Free Motion Slider.

Andy Belmas, the editor of this book. He is truly a patient man, and I am grateful for all the excellent suggestions he made along the way.

Candy Wiza, who is the most outgoing and approachable editor at Quilt Market.

Robert Best, who I found to be a great photographer and all around good guy.

All the staff at Krause Publications, thank you for your efforts on this project.

Introduction

I still remember completing my first quilt top in 1991. It was a small, wall-hanging sized quilt that I pieced by machine. I draped the quilt top over a chair, and then stared at the last page of the quilt instructions which read, "Quilt as desired." I was in trouble. I had been sewing for 25 years, but I had no quilting experience. So I quilted it by machine, sewing straight lines without a walking foot. Disappointed, I packed the wall hanging away.

A year later, my sister made arrangements for us to attend an upcoming quilt show. At exactly 10:00 AM on the day of the quilt show, the doors opened to what would become my favorite sewing passion. I was stunned at how many quilts were quilted using a sewing machine.

I couldn't get enough quilting, and my mother gave me the gift of a Pfaff machine. Several years and many quilts later, I am still captured by the art of quilting. I love every quilt I see, and the quilters who make them.

New tools and technologies have turned quilting into an activity that everyone can enjoy. We don't have to be trained artists or mathematicians to produce beautiful quilts in a reasonable amount of time.

This is the book I was looking for when I first started quilting. I hope this book will motivate you to complete the many tops that are waiting to be made into the lovely quilts they were meant to be.

Table of Contents

SECTION THREE: Projects...............80

Technical Aspects of Quilting

With stitch-in-the-ditch, the pieced fabric is emphasized with minimal surface texture.

Straight-line quilting adds a strong geometric texture.

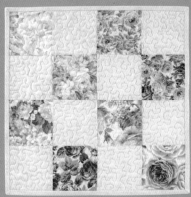

Meandering blends all of the fabrics together and creates a graceful texture to the fabric surface.

In its simplest form, quilting is the sewing that holds the three quilt layers together: the quilt top, the batting and the backing. In its most complex form, quilting is the art of using thread and pattern to breathe life into the quilt surface. In this book, I will show you the techniques you need to become a quilter; from the practical to the artistic and everything in between.

Frequently Used Terms

Before we begin, review the following list of terms or phrases used frequently throughout the book.

All-over quilting pattern
A pattern used over a large area of a quilt or an entire quilt surface.

Binding
A narrow, folded strip of coordinating fabric that finishes the outer edges of a quilt. Adding the binding is the last step of a project, after the quilting is done.

Echo quilting
A line of quilting that traces an existing motif. Echo quilting can trace existing quilting, a piece in a block, an appliqué or an embroidery design.

Fat quarter
A piece of fabric measuring 18" x 21". When cutting $1/4$ yard of fabric from selvage to selvage, the cut is 9" wide. A fat quarter comes from a half-yard cut of fabric with an additional cut at the fold of the fabric.

Finished size
The size of a block or portion of a quilt after all the piecing has been completed.

Free-motion quilting
Popular quilting method in which the quilter disengages the feed dogs and moves the quilt sandwich in a random or marked sequence.

Fussy-cut
A fabric cutting technique that carefully cuts novelty print fabric. The cutting centers an image in a square of fabric.

Grain
Straight grain — parallel to selvage
Cross grain — selvage to selvage

Pin-basting
Securing the quilt layers prior to quilting with quality safety pins.

Quilt sandwich
A layer of backing fabric, a layer of batting and the quilt top which have been basted together to form a single unit.

Straight-line quilting
A quilting technique using a walking foot to feed the quilt sandwich through the machine as a single unit. A walking foot does not lend itself to curved quilting lines.

Strip
A single strip of fabric cut on the cross grain of the fabric (selvage edge to selvage edge).

Strip set
The piece created by sewing two or more strips together.

Tools

The Sewing Machine

While all sewing machines are able to quilt, some machines are more capable than others. Below are some steps to take to enable your sewing machine to run at its optimum level of performance.

Read Your Manual

Reacquaint yourself with threading, bobbin loading, and the exterior parts of your machine. If you have lost your manual, contact the manufacturer. Some manufacturers will mail copies to you or provide them on their web site.

Get Your Machine Serviced

Just as regular visits to the dentist help to keep your teeth healthy, your sewing machine needs annual visits to your local sewing machine dealer for cleaning, oiling and fine tuning.

Know How To Use Your Machine

Know how to change stitch length, adjust thread tension, lower feed dogs and change specialty feet.

Clean and Oil Your Machine

Know how to perform routine cleaning and oiling on your own machine. Learn to remove the needle plate to remove the excess lint. Quilting stirs up a great deal of lint. Replace your old cleaning brush to remove dust and lint from every crevice under the needle plate and around the bobbin.

Practice

Make several quilt sandwiches that are approximately 10" square. They do not need to be pin basted. Stack them up next to your sewing machine to use for practice or "warming up" before a quilt session. Practice adjusting thread tension.

Sewing-Machine Accessories

There are several sewing-machine accessories that are vital for machine quilting, and some accessories that are optional. The following accessories are required:

Walking Foot

(Called IDT on Pfaff machines.) In straight-line machine quilting, it is important that the quilt sandwich move through the machine as a single unit. A walking foot has a top layer of feed dogs which work in unison with the bottom feed dogs to both pull and push the three layers of the quilt as a single unit. The additional feed dogs help form uniform, flat stitches. Without a walking foot, the three layers shift irregularly when quilting. If you don't have one, your local sewing machine dealer can fit your machine with a suitable walking foot.

Free-Motion Quilting Foot

(Also called a darning foot.) In free-motion quilting, the feed dogs are disengaged, and the quilt sandwich is completely guided by the quilter. It is important to use a foot that allows a good view of the stitches and that allows the quilt to be moved smoothly. The free-motion quilting foot places downward pressure on the quilt layers as the needle rises. At the point where the needle has cleared the fabric, the darning foot releases its pressure, allowing the quilter to move the quilt sandwich along. Because this function occurs so quickly, we can move the quilt under the needle smoothly.

Quarter-Inch Foot

A specialty foot used primarily for piecing the quilt top. It is also used to attach the binding once the quilting is complete.

Extension Table

Provides a large, flat surface to the left of the sewing machine for quilters who do not have the benefit of a built-in cabinet. While it is possible to straight-line quilt the layers without the extension table, it is very difficult to free-motion quilt without one. Acrylic extension tables are readily available at sewing shops and online.

Edge Guide

(Also called a quilting bar.) In straight-line quilting, the edge guide determines where the next quilted line should go, letting us mark fewer lines on the quilt top. The guide bar is adjustable for various widths of quilting lines. Some guide bars attach directly to the walking foot, while others attach to the presser-foot holder. After marking and sewing a single straight line, the guide bar is aligned to the first line of sewing. Making sure that the guide bar traces the first line of sewing, the next line of quilting is sewn. This can be repeated for many rows. For accurate, proportioned results, it is best to mark at least every other row of required quilting.

Optional Accessories

Stitch Regulator

This new technology uses sensors to measure the front-to-back and side-to-side motion of the quilt layers during free-motion quilting. Stitch lengths are set into the regulator by the user. As the sensors detect movement, the regulator speeds up or slows down the needle pace to make every stitch the same pre-determined length. Once it is attached to your sewing machine, the stitch regulator maintains consistently sized stitches. This technology is a wonderful option for anyone struggling to obtain consistently sized stitches. It is necessary to visit your local sewing machine dealer for custom installation.

Single-Needle Plate

(Also called Straight-Stitch Needle Plate.)

Most sewing machines are manufactured to accommodate many types of sewing functions and decorative stitches. Therefore, the opening in the needle plate is rather large. A straight-stitch needle plate has a small opening for a single needle in the center position. As the needle pushes into the quilt sandwich, the small opening prevents fabric layers from getting pushed down, resulting in better stitches. It is easier on your machine's motor, too.

Mini Long-Arm Sewing Machine

If you are interested in purchasing a new sewing machine, you may wish to audition a machine that has an extra-long, extra-high arm. Those extra inches make a big difference on large projects. The larger span on the sewing machine bed is easier and faster to use if you have any hand or wrist weaknesses. These machines also come with an extension table, a walking foot, and a free-motion foot.

Notions

Scissors

All scissors are not alike. You need a sharp pair of scissors to clip threads close to the quilt top without cutting the fabric. Embroidery scissors or tweezers scissors with the rounded tips are the best for this purpose.

Gripping Devices

The fabrics and batting we use in quilts absorb moisture from the skin, and it can become a strain to move a large quilt smoothly when the hands or fingers slip on the surface. Using gripping tools, you will obtain more consistent results with less struggle and fatigue.

Gloves

There are generally two types of gloves: one type has little vinyl dots covering the finger and palm sections of the glove; another type has top halves of the fingers dipped in a lightweight polymer that feels rubbery. The type you choose depends on personal preference. Try them on in the store. Do not be fooled by "one size fits all." If you have arthritis or a hand/wrist injury that affects finger dexterity, use a glove that has the little vinyl dots, but make certain the glove fits perfectly.

Finger Gloves

Sized to fit over your fingers, individual finger gloves provide excellent control. They should not be so small that they cut off circulation, nor too big that they fall off while quilting.

Hint

Try wearing the individual finger gloves on one or two fingers of the left hand when piecing your quilts. You will be amazed at how much control you will have in feeding the fabric into the machine, especially at the starting point. I prefer one on my index finger.

Hand gloves are easier to put on and take off than individual finger gloves. If you have several thread changes in quick succession required for your quilt top, full gloves are the most suitable.

Hoop

Used for free-motion quilting, hoops are very helpful for anyone who has had serious hand injury or illness. All they take is a little pressure from any part of the hand, and you can control the quilt sandwich. To use a hoop, you must use an extension table or your machine needs to be built into a custom cabinet.

Basting Pins

Basting pins come in many sizes in both stainless steel and brass. The size of the safety pins is determined by the length of the shaft. The smaller the basting pin, the smaller the hole in the quilt top. Large, 1½" to 2" safety pins are generally too big, but can be used if you have trouble with finger strength and dexterity. Size 1 basting pins have a 1" shaft and are the most versatile–they are well suited for all commercial fabrics using any type of batting. Size 0 basting pins (the shaft is ¾" to ⅞" long) leave a smaller hole, but are more difficult to use with a high-loft batting. They are the best pins to use on batiks and other tightly woven fabrics with a low-loft batting. Avoid purchasing regular safety pins, since they can have dull points or burrs. Never sew over a basting pin. They must be removed as you quilt.

Kwik Klip

This notion helps close the basting pins quickly and safely once they have been inserted into the quilt. When pin-basting a quilt, first insert all of the pins into the quilt layers, and then come back and close them with the Kwik Klip.

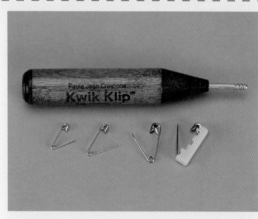

Organize your basting pins by size. Once they have been removed from the quilt, store them open. The pin basting step in subsequent quilts will go much faster if you don't have to stop to open every pin. Plastic pin grips are available for the size 1 basting pins. They make gripping the pins much easier, especially for arthritic fingers. Above the basting pins is a Kwik Klip.

Masking Tape, Spring Clamps or Table Cloth Grips

Masking tape is used to secure backing fabric to the table when layering a small, wall-hanging-sized quilt sandwich. Yellow painter's masking tape that is 1" wide works best. The blue painter's tape should be avoided. Spring clamps are used when layering and pin basting large projects. Test out various sizes at your home improvement store to determine if they are too hard for you to open. Also make sure they will fit your table top. Table cloth clips are easy to use, but don't fit every table.

Rotary Cutting Ruler

I prefer a 24" x 6" rotary cutting ruler for marking lines for straight-line quilting.

Seam Ripper

Sad, but true; we all make mistakes. A sharp seam ripper will enable you to cut threads very quickly without putting undue stress on the quilt layers.

Free-Motion Slider

This sturdy sheet of Teflon is taped onto the sewing machine bed. It allows the quilt layers to glide easily during free-motion quilting. The user can quilt for longer periods of time with less fatigue. This is a good tool for anyone with arthritis or other hand injury.

High-Quality Office Chair

Good posture for both straight-line and free-motion quilting requires you to be elevated higher than standard chairs allow. Many office chairs are designed to be raised and lowered by the user to adjust for various heights.

Thread

The green thread to the far left is 100-weight silk thread by YLI. The next two eggshell-colored threads are 100% cotton by Mettler. The thread in the center is a 40-weight thread, while the thread to its left is a 50-weight thread. The two strands of blue/green variegated threads on the right are 100% cotton threads by Sulky. The strand to the far right is 12 weight, while the thread to its left is 30 weight.

Some quilters have enormous fabric stashes. I have a thread collection that my husband insists will last me the rest of my life. What does he know?

The weight of the thread refers to the thickness of the individual strands that are twisted together to make the thread. The heaviest threads use the lowest numbers. As the number gets higher, the weight becomes finer. With a little experience, all threads are suitable for some type of machine quilting. If you are just getting started in machine quilting, the 30-weight and the 40-weight cotton and polyester threads are the easiest to use, and all can be used in the bobbin.

The heavier-weight threads are the best threads to use with a high-loft batting where a finer thread would tend to get lost in the loft. Heavier-weight threads work very well for straight-line quilting or large free-motion patterns. The lighter-weight threads are best suited for stippling since they are less bulky for tiny stitches. The mid-weight threads are suitable for most straight-line and free-motion patterns.

Tip

Sometimes I find a thread I love, and I cannot resist purchasing it. Then I find fabric to match the thread. If looking for specific colors, consider buying the quilting thread first, and then find the fabric.

100% Cotton

Available in an enormous variety of colors and weights. All cotton threads can be used in the bobbin, so they are easy to use. When making a quilt that will be heavily used, choose cotton thread. It is soft to the touch, readily available, strong, and long lasting.

Rayon

Widely available for home-embroidery machines. Rayon has a beautiful sheen and is available in every color imaginable. It is not a strong thread, and therefore not as suitable as cotton for utilitarian quilts. Not all rayon thread can be used in the bobbin. If you find a rayon thread that is a suitable choice for your quilt top, but cannot be used in the bobbin, use a fine-weight bobbin thread instead.

Metallic

Metallic threads now come in many colors and weights. Metallic threads are not appropriate for the bobbin since they are prone to shredding. Therefore, you must use an embroidery bobbin thread or a different lightweight thread in the bobbin (cotton, silk or lightweight polyester). Experiment with your machine to determine the best bobbin thread and tension for smooth quilting. When using a metallic thread, maintain a slower stitch speed to prevent thread breakage.

Silk

While expensive, silk threads produce remarkable results. They are durable and strong at all weights and can be used in the bobbin. The finest weight silk threads require that the bobbin tension be increased slightly in order to get the best thread tension.

Polyester

Polyester thread comes in all colors, and it's strong, durable and easy to use. Polyester does not shrink when laundered. For the machine quilter, the heavier weight polyester threads provide vibrant color that seems to float on the surface. It can easily be used in the bobbin.

Monofilament

Invisible thread made of nylon or polyester; comes in two shades: clear and smoke. Popular for novice quilters because it hides imperfect stitches. It is not suitable for the bobbin, so a fine-weight thread must be used in the bobbin.

I use monofilament thread for some sewing, but never for quilting. Because the mono-filament thread is fine and invisible, the stitches can look less like quilting and more like hole-punching on light fabrics.

Needles

Always, always, always insert a new needle before starting a quilt. Dull needles cause skipped stitches. You may need more than one new needle to quilt an entire project. You can usually hear when a needle is dull because it makes a "thunking" sound as it tries to get through all of the quilt layers.

There are several needle types and sizes suitable for machine quilting. Choosing the correct needle is simple; the decision is determined by your thread choice.

Below are some general guidelines for selecting machine needles.

Quilting Needles

Very sharp and designed to sew through multiple layers of fabric, quilting needles work well with fine to mid-weight cotton or polyester threads. Use a size 75 needle for the lightweight threads and a size 90 needle for mid-weight threads. Excellent for straight-line quilting with cotton or polyester threads.

Embroidery Needles

These needles are designed to stitch delicate rayon thread through dense layers at high speeds. Therefore, they are an excellent choice for silk and rayon threads.

Topstitch Needles

The most versatile free-motion quilting needles. Extremely sharp with very large eyes, enabling thread to move through easily at high speeds. If you are experiencing repeated thread

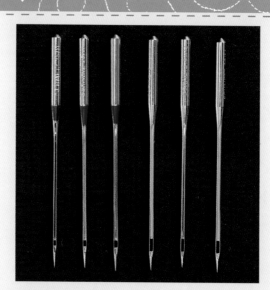

The needles shown here from left to right include:

Size 75 Quilting Needle; Size 75 Embroidery Needle; Size 90 Embroidery Needle; Size 90 Metallic Needle; Size 80 Topstitch Needle; Size 90 Topstitch Needle. Look at the eyes of each needle and note the range of sizes.

breakage, consider using a topstitch needle. The size 90 topstitch needle works under many conditions for every type of thread, so keep a supply of these handy. Some quilters use topstitch needles almost exclusively. If quilting a tight weave fabric, such as a batik, use a size 80 topstitch needle.

Metallic Needles

Like the topstitch needle, these have a very large eye. They also have a large groove so the thread can be sewn with less friction and less shredding.

Preparing the Layers

Each layer of your quilt sandwich needs some individual attention before pin basting them into a single unit. Your efforts in this phase of the quilting process will reward you with a quilt that hangs flat or drapes gracefully.

The Quilt Top

Unless you frantically finished a quilt top the night before you want to present it as a gift, it is likely that there have been several days (weeks, months, or even years) since you finished your quilt top. It is time to take a critical look at it, and fix any significant issues.

Begin by pressing the entire quilt top without using steam. You are not trying to re-shape the quilt top. You are only making sure every seam is pressed in the direction you intended. Check both the front and the back of the quilt top. Minor imperfections can be absorbed during the quilting process. But the major flaws need to be corrected now.

Marking

For the purposes of accuracy, most straight-line quilting designs and some free-motion patterns require some marking. A thorough knowledge of marking techniques can be useful to the novice quilter.

Before basting the quilt layers together, decide which quilting pattern you will be using. If the quilting pattern you plan to sew requires any marking, now is the time to complete this step. Once the quilt sandwich is basted, it is very difficult to mark.

There is a large variety of marking tools available today.

Do not use typical graphite pencils to mark. In some cases, the pencil lines will not wash out. There are many better ways to mark the fabric.

Pencils

There is a huge variety of marking pencils for quilt surfaces. They usually come in white, gray scale, or primary colors. Some pencils wear off over time, and others require laundering. Always follow the manufacturer's instructions.

Wash-Away Markers

Blue markers that wash away with a simple spray of water or laundering. In some cases, the blue markers are packaged with a purple marker that is not suitable for quilting, as the lines disappear long before the quilting even begins. Make sure you are using the correct marker.

Soap Stone

Marks a white line of soap on quilts that rinses away in the laundry.

Chalk

There are two types of chalk markers. One is a pad of loose chalk that, when tapped on a stencil, leaves behind chalk lines. Though dusty, it is a fast way to mark stencils. A light spray starch will hold the marks longer. Chalk rollers are also available. The loose chalk is expelled from the container as the metal wheel rolls along the fabric. These make thin, precise lines for straight-line quilting on small projects.

Marking Sprays

Designed to be used with stencils. Just place the stencil on the quilt, and spray the surface. As the spray dries, it leaves behind a white tracing of the stencil. The marks wash away in the laundry.

Tracing Paper

Trace the quilting design on a single sheet of tracing paper, pin several sheets together with the traced design on top and stitch through all paper layers using an unthreaded machine. Pin the individual tracings onto the quilt surface, thread the machine, and then sew over the paper and quilt sandwich. After quilting, the paper is easily torn away.

Interfacing and Temporary Spray Adhesive

Favorite novelty images such as stars and hearts can be drawn on interfacing. Each image is cut out from the interfacing, then lightly sprayed with a temporary spray adhesive. Simply press each cut-out onto the quilt surface. Free-motion quilt around the cut-out image, then remove. Templates can be reused several times.

Easy Mark

A white marking tool that resembles a large crayon or a square tailor's chalk. It vanishes with heat. While a finished quilt surface is never pressed, merely holding the hot iron ¼" above the quilt surface provides enough heat to remove the marks.

Stencils

Beautiful stencils are available in continuous line designs for machine quilting. The stencils include labels that guide you in the direction the quilting needs to take.

Cookie Cutters

I use these to trace recognizable line drawings onto novelty prints. Since I don't bake much anymore, I find cookie cutters far more useful in my sewing room.

Plastic Template Sheets

These wonderful sheets aren't just for appliqué patterns. They can help you copy a line design and place the image anywhere on the quilt.

Preparing the Backing Fabric

The backing fabric is the backbone of your quilt. Because the backing is usually a solid piece of fabric with few or no seams, it provides stability over the life of the quilt. If the backing is heavily pieced, it is advisable to use a dense quilting pattern that will add stability to both the front and the back of the quilt.

Beginning quilters often wonder what to choose when selecting the backing fabric. Should it be the same as the borders or background fabric? Should it be lighter or darker in color? There is no right or wrong answer here. Use what you love. But if you are worried about imperfections showing on the back, consider using a busy backing fabric. Use something that includes the colors found in your quilting threads, as well as your bobbin thread selection. A busy fabric will hide all of the little stitch imperfections.

No matter how large or small the quilt top, the backing fabric should be cut or pieced so that it is 2" to 4" larger than the quilt top around all sides. Commercial patterns take this necessity into consideration when specifying yardage. If you have altered the size of a pattern, or have created a pattern of your own, make sure to calculate the backing fabric to accommodate the overhang.

When working on a quilt that is larger than the width of the backing fabric, the backing will need to be pieced. Before cutting the backing fabric, make sure to trim away all of the selvage edges. Selvage edges never belong in a quilt.

Piece the backing sections according to the pattern directions using a ⅝" seam. Because

A pieced backing is a great way to use up scraps of fabric.

This is the back of a quilt which has been densely quilted using three different colors in the bobbin.

you quilt from the top, it is impossible to know what part of the actual backing seams will become stitched. The wider seam is strong and secure, regardless of where the quilting lines end up. Press the seams open to spread the extra layers evenly across the backing.

This extra backing fabric beyond the quilt top is needed to maintain a firm, consistent hold on the quilt while the borders and edges are stitched. The backing is the seafoam colored batik fabric.

Hint

When first starting out, purchase pre-packaged batting. Make sure to read everything printed on the packaging. Save the printed instructions from the packaging in a folder and attach your own notes to the packaging regarding what worked best for your project. Over time, your collection of batting notes will be sufficient to purchase your favorite batting off the roll.

Batting

A high-quality batting will add surface texture by "puffing" between stitching lines, and it will drape evenly, provide warmth, and stand the test of time and wear. It must survive a gentle laundering process, and it must be easy to sew.

Batting can be purchased off a roll or pre-packed by size. With pre-packaged batting, you know exactly what you are getting. The packaging advises you about washing instructions, shrinkage, maximum distance between stitches and fiber content. When the batting is first removed from its package, it can be a bit of a tussle to smooth it into a flat layer–just unfold it and let it hang for a couple of days. Do not spray the batting with water unless recommended by the manufacturer.

Many quilt shops provide batting on a roll. Because the batting is cut to exact specifications, there is less waste, and the batting lays flat directly off the roll. Unfortunately, there is no packaging information. Before you buy, identify the manufacturer, the fiber content, and the weight of the batting from the retailer. You can visit the web site of any manufacturer to obtain the information typically located on the packaging. The resource section in the back of this book includes a list of web sites for several batting manufacturers.

Avoid purchasing any batting that has no source of origin, even if the price is economical.

100% Cotton

Cotton is a natural fiber used by many quilters. It is available in its natural color, bleached white or dyed black. Various manufacturers offer several weights of 100% cotton batting. There can be between 1% to 5% shrinkage of the quilt after it has been laundered, but the exact information is located on the packaging. 100% cotton batting tends to lose its puff and gets flatter with time and wear. But those of us who love that "instant" antique look can't resist the texture this batting brings to our quilts.

100% Polyester

This popular batting comes from a man-made fiber, and gives a very puffy look to the finished quilt. They come in a variety of lofts. Polyester battings do not shrink, never lose their loft, and stay puffy despite heavy use and many washings. Consider using a low-loft polyester batting when making place mats. Flat place mats will result in safer surfaces for stemware.

Cotton/Polyester Blends

The best of both worlds: puff and cotton properties. Some of these blends can be pre-washed, and therefore pre-shrunk. Directions for pre-washing are found on the packaging. These blended battings sew beautifully with our domestic sewing machines, and provide the quilt with wonderful drape.

Wool

Provides the most warmth for a bed quilt without weight. Loft retention is good, and wool batting is quite durable. Wool batting will shrink somewhat when laundered, but some can be pre-washed. Quilts made using wool batting drape gracefully.

Fusible Batting

Available on some polyester battings, fusible batting can be fused directly to the quilt top, eliminating the basting step. This option is suitable for smaller projects, but cumbersome for larger quilts.

Layering the Quilt Sandwich

The straight grain, parallel to the selvage, has very little give to it.

The cross grain, selvage to selvage, has some give and stretch to it.

Space the tape every 4" to 6".

The treatment of the backing fabric is the most important part of the layering process in machine quilting. The backing fabric must be as taut as possible without over-stretching the fabric when pin basting. The most frequent mistake novice quilters make in this step is failing to secure the backing fabric taut enough to the table. Following are two examples of this layering process. The first example is of a small project. The second example is a full-sized bed quilt that shows how the layering process is completed when the quilt top is larger than the table top, and therefore, must be pin basted in sections.

Layering a Small Quilt

Most wall hangings are small enough to fit on a table top and are the easiest to layer into a quilt sandwich.

Since the wall hanging is small, the backing fabric usually does not need to be pieced. In this example, the backing fabric has been cut to fit the size of the quilt top, with enough excess fabric to maintain the additional overage all the way around. The selvage edge has already been cut away.

1 Place the backing fabric on the table with the wrong side up.

2 Find the straight grain of the fabric by trying to stretch the fabric.

3 Beginning on one of the straight grain sides, secure it to the table with masking tape.

4 Working now on the opposite side of the backing fabric, secure the tape to the fabric, and pull the fabric taut. Since you are now pulling against the cross grain of the fabric, there will be a surprising amount of give. Finish securing the second side of the backing to the table working from the center out to each side.

5 Move to one of the remaining unsecured sides. Starting in the center, secure the tape to the fabric and pull the fabric out from the center until half of the puckering in the center disappears. Secure the final side by continuing to smooth out any remaining puckering.

6 Check to make sure that the backing is taut by moving your hand firmly across it.

Hint

Don't worry about over-stretching the fabric. If you pull too tight, the masking tape will release from either the fabric or the table, preventing over-stretching.

4

All commercial fabrics have plenty of ease in the cross grain of the fabric. It will feel like you are stretching the fabric, but that stretch is OK.

5

The four corners will often appear puckered. This is acceptable and is caused by the tension the fabric is under.

6

At first you might think the backing fabric has been over-stretched. But notice how much ease is still left in the fabric when a hand is moved across it.

9

The pins should not be more than 4" apart.

7 Place the layer of batting over the backing fabric. The batting should not be stretched, nor should it be too loose. The batting should lie very flat with absolutely no puckers or folds. The batting does not need to be secured separately.

8 Spread your quilt top over the batting.

9 When you are satisfied that the quilt is taut against the batting, insert the basting pins making sure to capture all three layers. Close the pins.

10 Remove the masking tape. The quilt will appear to shrink. When this sandwich is quilted both the top and the backing will be flat!

Hint

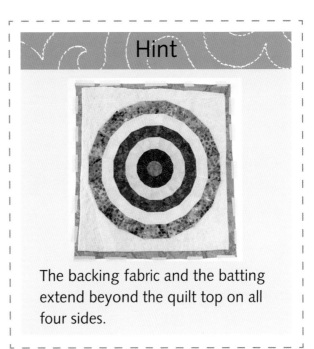

The backing fabric and the batting extend beyond the quilt top on all four sides.

Layering a Large Quilt

Most sewing tables are 40" x 72". Any quilt larger than crib sized will not fit on the standard cutting table for the purpose of basting the layers, so the quilt has to be pin basted in sections. It is tempting to get a larger table, or push two tables together. However, most people are not tall enough to reach over the width of two tables to secure basting pins. The following basting method is possible for anyone to complete alone.

Whatever size table is available to you, make sure you can access all four sides. A standard-sized lap quilt can be completed in two sections, while a twin-sized quilt will take up to four sections. Both the king- and queen-sized quilts will take up to six sections to fully pin baste on a standard size 30" x 72" table.

In the following example, the selvage edges have been cut away and the backing fabric has been pieced. It is a full-sized quilt, and on this small table, it will be pin basted in six sections. At any given time, two or three sides of the table will not lend themselves to tape, so clamps need to be used instead. You need to find clamps that fit your table. I use a combination of plastic picnic tablecloth grips and spring clamps from a home improvement store. You might also consider the large metal paper clamps available from an office supply store.

1 Place the backing fabric on the table with the wrong side up so a corner of it is on the table and there is considerable overhang on two sides.

One side at a time, secure the backing to the table using the spring clamps.

2 Beginning on the top edge (straight of grain), secure the first side of the backing fabric to the table with clamps. For a large quilt, the straight grain of the fabric will almost always be the top edge or bottom edge of the backing. Space the clamps about every 8" to 10". Then secure the opposite side starting in the center of the table and working out to each end. Make sure to pull the fabric taut as you clamp it to the table.

4

5

Because there are now three layers of the quilt sandwich under tension, the clamps provide the best stability for holding the quilt sandwich to the table.

3 Check that ease is still left in the fabric when your hand is moved across the surface of the backing fabric. (See Step 6 of "Layering a Small Quilt.")

4 Smooth the layer of batting over the backing fabric. The batting will lay over the clamps on two sides.

5 Spread the quilt top over the batting. Make sure to leave 3" - 4" of backing and batting around the top and side edges. The quilt top will lay over the clamps on two sides. Up through this step, only the backing remains clamped to the table.

6 When you are satisfied that the quilt is taut against the batting, insert the basting pins. (See Step 9 of "Layering a Small Quilt.")

7 When all of the basting pins have been closed, remove the clamps. Move the quilt layers on the table to the next section to be basted. Starting with the long side that has already been pin basted, clamp the quilt sandwich to the table, pulling the sandwich taut as you add clamps. If you see the quilt top start to buckle, you have stretched too much. The backing may buckle somewhat, but the quilt top must be flat.

8 Gently fold the quilt top and batting layers up and over to rest on the clamps that are securing the first section to the table. Only the backing fabric remains fully exposed on the table.

9 Starting on the longest unsecured side, pull the backing taut at the center, clamp it to the table and work out to each end.

10 Clamp the remaining ends.

8

Be careful not to stretch the batting in this step.

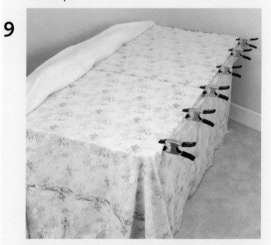

9

Check the backing fabric where the last line of safety pins ended to make sure that the backing is as taut in the center of the quilt as it is along the edges of the table.

10

11

Bring the clamps to the top to help secure the batting and backing. There is so much fabric, the clamps help secure all of the layers as you work your way around the table.

11 Carefully smooth your batting over the exposed backing. Place the quilt top over the exposed batting as you did in Steps 4 and 5 of the first section of the quilt. Bring the clamps to the top to help secure the batting and backing. Once all of the layers are taut, pin baste this section.

Once the pins have been closed, repeat Steps 7 through 11 on the remaining sections. Fully pin basted, the layers are ready to be turned into a quilt!

Setting Up Your Quilting Space

When quilting, the space where you work can make a significant difference in your enjoyment of quilting and the outcome of your project.

1 Set your sewing machine and extension table on a smooth surface. While you will only be quilting a small section at a time, the quilt needs to move freely on the work surface as you go.

2 Create a sizable work space for yourself. On medium and large projects, use two tables set up in an "L" shape so that the weight of the quilt will be spread out on the table surface.

3 Quilting is more comfortable if you are seated higher than standard-chair height. An adjustable chair places less strain on your neck and lower back.

4 When seated, center your body to the needle of the machine.

5 Make sure you have excellent lighting, especially when working with dark threads on dark fabrics.

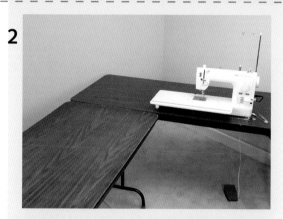

2

3

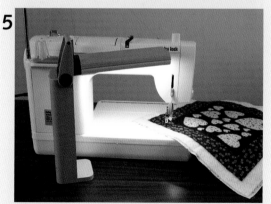

5

Additional lighting added to the rear of the sewing machine.

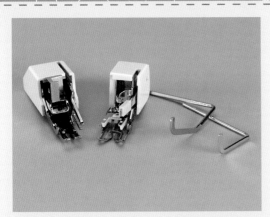

Two typical walking feet. To the right are guide bars that fit in the walking foot or presser-foot holder.

Rest elbows comfortably at the sides, place hands on either side of the needle, slightly in front of it. When ready to reposition the hands, stop the machine, move the hands, then resume sewing. Straight lines become crooked lines when the hands are removed while the needle is still moving.

Straight-Line Quilting

In straight-line machine quilting, the stitch length and direction of stitches are determined by the machine. A "walking foot" replaces the standard presser foot to ensure that the three quilt layers move through the machine as a single unit.

Quilting a straight line requires a slower speed than the speed you sewed the quilt-top pieces. A medium speed gives the walking foot and the bottom feed dogs ample opportunity to grab and move the quilt sandwich.

No sewing machine is engineered to pull your quilt up off the floor, over the tabletop and into the machine. Guiding the quilt sandwich is your responsibility. Make sure there are no obstructions in the way.

Plan the order you will sew your lines in advance. You can start in the center and work out to the sides, or you can begin on one side and finish at the other. The choice is often dictated by the pattern. Sewing from the center out is often the best option.

The best posture for straight-line quilting has to do with guiding the quilt sandwich towards the machine.

Prepare the Machine

Follow these steps to prepare your machine for straight-line quilting.

1 Attach the walking foot.

2 Make sure the stitch is set for straight-line sewing with the needle in the center position.

3 If one is available for your machine, insert the single-needle plate.

4 Set the stitch length for 2.5. This is often the default setting for computerized machines. It is a standard, medium-length stitch.

5 Thread the machine.

Free-Motion Quilting

In free-motion machine quilting, the stitch length and direction of stitches are determined by the quilter. The three quilt layers move through the machine in all directions as a single unit completely under your control. To help the machine create smooth stitches, we attach a darning foot or a free-motion foot.

There are generally two postures for free-motion machine quilting. They both have to do with how you will prefer to move the quilt sandwich. See photos at right. Notice that the hands are placed on both sides of the needle.

(Note: I always quilt using some type of gripping gloves. However, for the purpose of demonstration, gloves were not used.)

The front left foot is a darning foot. The remaining four feet are free-motion quilting feet.

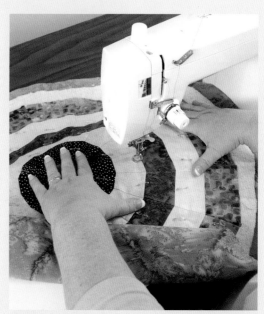

In the first position, the hands or fingers grip the quilt on either side of the needle. The elbows rest comfortably at the sides, and the quilt is moved by the forearms and upper arms, ideal for larger free-motion stitch patterns.

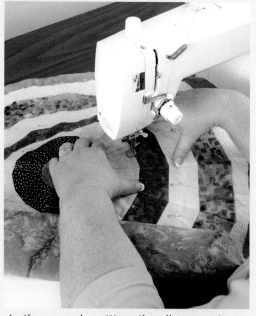

In the second position, the elbows rest on the edge of the table surface or the extension table. The quilt layers are moved by the finger tips and wrists, ideal for smaller free-motion stitch patterns.

Prepare the Machine

Follow these steps to prepare your machine for free-motion quilting.

1 Attach the free-motion foot or darning foot.

2 Lower the feed dogs. It is not necessary to set the stitch length. Once the feed dogs are lowered, the stitch length is determined by the quilter.

3 Make sure the stitch is set for straight-line sewing with the needle in the center position.

4 If one is available for your machine, insert the single-needle plate.

5 Thread the machine.

Poor hand position results in poor stitches and pattern formation.

Hint

In some machines, the feed dogs do not lower. Instead, a square plate is attached to cover the feed dogs. These covers are often cumbersome. Instead, consider using the Free-Motion Slider. It is not bothered by the feed dogs and will enable you to move your quilt sandwich freely.

Thread Tension

Stitches are formed when the needle forces the top thread through the fabric layers, all the way down into the bobbin. The bobbin spins in its casing and catches the needle thread. As the take-up lever rises, it draws up the excess top thread, and a single stitch is formed. Ideally, the final "crossing" of the top thread and the bobbin thread occurs in the exact center of the quilt sandwich. The bobbin thread should not be seen from the top, and the top thread should not be seen from the bottom.

When using a medium- to heavy-weight thread and a thin batting, one of the threads will likely appear on its opposite surface of the quilt. Your goal is to adjust the tension to allow the top thread to barely show on the bottom surface. Lightweight threads can be tricky to balance; sometimes the bobbin case needs to be tightened slightly. Beginners should learn to balance tension with cotton or polyester threads.

Thread tension can be tricky, don't lose patience at this point. Often it is easier to feel poor thread tension with your fingers than to see it. After sewing out some test lines, move your fingertips over the stitch lines on both sides of the quilt sandwich. If both lines feel smooth, even though a tiny part of the top thread shows on the bottom, good job!

Balancing Thread Tension

Starting with a 10"-square quilt sandwich, sew several lines using the walking foot. Stop at the end of each line to check thread tension.

On the following page are three examples of **straight-line quilting** with the wrong side folded over on the top so you can see the front and the back of each line of stitching.

The line on the left shows correct thread tension. The top thread (white) and bobbin thread (orange) cross one another inside of the quilt sandwich.

In the middle line of stitching, the bobbin thread appears on the top, indicating that the top thread tension is too high. Loosen the thread tension only a half number, and sew another line. Keep repeating this step until the bobbin thread disappears from the quilt top.

In the line of stitching to the right, the top surface looks good, but the needle thread appears on the bottom. In this example the top tension is too low. Raise the thread tension a half number, and sew another line. Repeat this step until the top thread disappears from the bottom.

To check tension for **free-motion quilting**, prepare another 10"-square quilt sandwich. Holding on to the thread tails, lower the presser foot, and start to move the quilt sandwich. Do

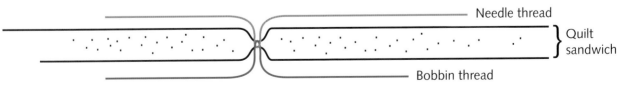

Ideally, tension is set so the needle thread (red) interlocks with the bobbin thread (green) in the batting, between the two layers of fabric.

Balancing tension for straight-line quilting.

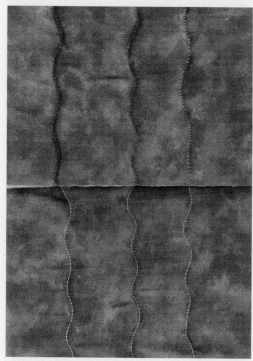

Balancing tension for free-motion quilting.

not worry about stitch length or pattern formation. After five or six stitches, release the thread tails. Concentrate on moving the quilt sandwich in gentle waves.

After sewing a few waves, stop and check the thread tension. Thread tension is easier to achieve in straight-line quilting because the feed dogs and presser foot work together to form even, flat stitches. With a little patience and practice, you can achieve balanced thread tension in free-motion quilting.

Continue to adjust the thread tension until you find a happy balance. If there is going to be a problem with thread tension, it will show up on the back of the quilt on sharply curved lines.

With some threads, you may have to let a tiny bit of the top thread show on the backing surface. Avoid allowing the bobbin thread to show on the quilt top. Busy backing fabric can be used to hide little imperfections.

After several failed attempts at trying to achieve balanced thread tension in free-motion quilting, it may be necessary to repeat a few steps.

1 Check to see that the machine is lint free.

2 Check the owner's manual to make sure your machine is properly set up for free-motion sewing.

3 Remove the bobbin from the bobbin case, re-thread the bobbin and the machine from scratch, and re-insert the bobbin case. If the thread has jumped out of even one thread guide, it will be very difficult to balance the thread tension.

4 Make sure you are using the same cotton or polyester thread in the bobbin and needle. Once you get used to setting thread tension, you can experiment with different threads.

5 Begin again by drawing up the bobbin thread, lowering the presser foot and holding on to the thread tails as you form the first several stitches.

6 Place a size 90 topstitch needle in the machine.

NOTE If you have tried all these corrective steps and are still not successful, then stop. Your machine may need a visit to your machine dealer for a thorough cleaning and oiling. It is possible that the timing is off or another moving part is out of alignment. It can be off enough to affect free-motion quilting while still working for other functions. Be sure to explain on the repair receipt that you wish to use your machine for free-motion quilting. If your machine cannot form free-motion stitches, the dealer can help you find a machine (new or used) in your price range. If you are in the market for an updated machine, take small quilt sandwiches to the dealer and make sure that the machine performs for you.

Hint

The most common mistake novice free-motion quilters make is that after raising the bobbin thread to the top, they forget to lower the presser foot. A thread knot is the outcome, and needs to be cut away from the machine.

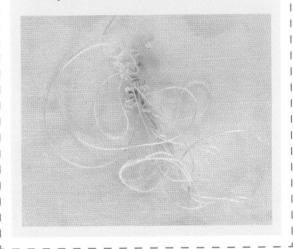

Starting and ending lines of quilting are very similar in both straight-line and free-motion quilting. The following directions apply to both quilting techniques.

To Begin a Quilting Line

1 Place the quilt sandwich under the needle at the part where your first line of stitching begins. To avoid thread knots on the back of the quilt, it is necessary to bring the bobbin thread to the top of the quilt. Holding on to the needle thread with your left hand, make one full turn with the fly wheel, taking the needle down through all layers to pick up the bobbin thread. Keep turning the fly wheel until the take-up lever is in its highest position.

2 Slowly pull the quilt a few inches away from the needle and take hold of the top thread. Use the top thread to bring the bobbin thread up to the surface of the quilt.

Hint

Whenever possible, start and stop in the seams. The loft from the batting at the seams will hide the location where you started and ended.

3 Take a firm hold of both thread ends and place the quilt back to its starting position. Lower the presser foot.

In straight-line quilting, lower the stitch length to .5. Keep holding the thread tails and sew seven or eight tiny stitches.

In free-motion quilting, hold the thread tails, and sew seven or eight tiny stitches, guiding the quilt very slowly.

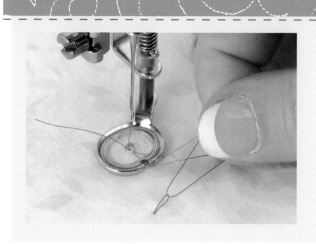

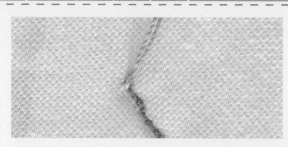

Secure the thread ends with tiny stitches. Do not sew forward and reverse to secure the thread ends since this will add bulk at every location on the quilt where you started and stopped.

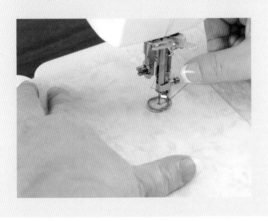
4 Once the thread ends are secure, sew a few stitches until the thread ends can be snipped off. Be careful not to cut the quilt top.

5 Reposition your hands to guide the quilt layers through the machine. Once you have stitched far enough so that your hands need to be repositioned, stop the machine. One at a time, reposition the hands, and begin again. Don't keep sewing while the hands are being repositioned. No matter how small your quilt is, the machine needs you to guide the quilt sandwich 100% of the time.

To End a Quilting Line

1 As you approach the end of a stitching line, slow down.

2 About ¼" away from the ending, sew five to eight tiny stitches to the end of the line. It should look exactly like you started.

3 Raise the presser foot and pull the quilt away. Clip the threads.

When the Thread Runs Out

If the bobbin thread runs out, make sure to brush away all of the lint from the bobbin housing before placing in a full bobbin. Quilting produces lots of lint!

1 Cut both the bobbin and top threads close to the quilt top.

2 Once a filled bobbin or new spool of thread has been threaded through the machine, place the quilt back under the needle on the same stitching line ½" before the threads were clipped.

3 Bring the bobbin thread to the top of the quilt (see page 37).

4 Sew about 8 to 10 tiny stitches directly over the last half inch of the former line.

5 Continue quilting. Snip off the thread tails when they are easily accessible.

Practice Exercises

Straight-Line Practice

Once good thread tension has been established, it is helpful to sew several straight lines on another 10"-square sandwich to get used to the walking foot. Because the machine determines stitch length, and the direction is always forward in a straight line, little additional practice is necessary. Remember to maintain a medium speed, and never reposition the hands while the needle is moving. Your skill level will rise very quickly when applied to projects.

Free-Motion Practice

Free-motion quilting requires that you determine the direction you are sewing. The speed at which you quilt is a personal preference. The goal is to have consistently sized stitches, which takes some practice. The rate at which the needle is moving, combined with the pace at which you move the quilt sandwich, determines stitch length. The slower the needle rate, and the faster you move the quilt sandwich, the larger the stitches will be. The faster the needle rate, and the slower you move the quilt sandwich, the smaller the stitches will be. Your goal is to find balance between the movement of the quilt and the speed of the machine.

When free-motion quilting, you focus on rhythm and direction. You might feel frustrated trying to do two unfamiliar tasks at the same time. The following practice exercises concentrate on only one skill at a time. With practice, you will be able to apply both skills simultaneously.

The stitch regulator (see page 11) is fast becoming a popular machine accessory for those who have been frustrated trying to maintain a consistent stitch length. However, it is possible to maintain rhythm and graceful pattern formation without a regulator. Be patient with yourself. Let yourself make mistakes. In the beginning it is important that you just keep sewing.

Move through the exercises in order, and repeat as necessary. Start by preparing six 10"-square quilt sandwiches. Do not worry about pin basting. The 10" squares can be almost any commercial fabric. Avoid batiks or tightly-woven, hand-dyed fabrics for the practice exercises. Make sure you have followed the steps on pages 32 through 36 on machine set-up and thread tension.

Practice Exercise #1

1 Starting on an upper edge, draw the bobbin thread to the top. Secure the thread as described on page 37, and then clip the thread tails.

2 Begin to move the layers in gentle wavy lines. Your goal is to find a good working rhythm between the speed of your machine and the movement of the quilt layers. Do not worry about forming a recognizable quilting pattern.

Concentrate on the following:

- Focus only on where you are going.
- Do not watch the stitches forming, and do not focus on the needle while it is moving. Look only at where you want your upcoming stitches to be.
- Practice using a moderate machine speed. Increase and decrease the speed of your movement to get used to the motion.
- When it is time to reposition the hands on either side of the needle, stop the machine, reposition the hands, and then continue to quilt. Resist the urge to reposition the hands while the needle is still moving.

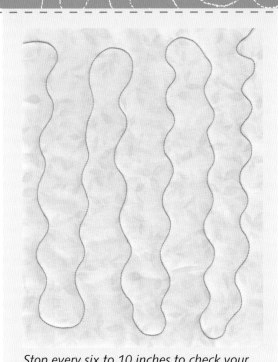

Stop every six to 10 inches to check your stitch length. Do you need to increase or decrease the speed of the machine? Perhaps you may need to increase or decrease the pace at which you move the quilt.

Hint

It is tempting to watch the stitches coming from your machine to check them for length and consistency. It is a bad habit. Concentrate on where you are going, not where you've been.

By sewing these lines in a circular fashion, you are practicing each pattern in every direction.

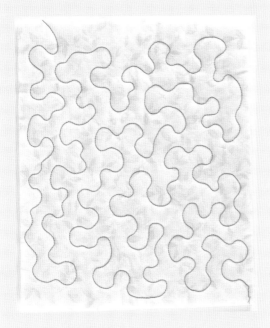

Practice Exercise #2

This exercise is much like learning to write in grade school. The repetition forms muscle memory and the confidence to move the quilt sandwich in any direction.

1 Sew circular lines of waves, loops, crescents and curves. Focus on shapes, not rhythm. Ignore the imperfections. Your rhythm will return as you become more comfortable with the shapes and the direction you are sewing. Be patient with yourself. You are learning to maintain rhythm and focus on direction at the same time. Keep sewing your favorite lines over and over until you get your rhythm back.

Practice Exercise #3

Let's take a look at forming the most popular free-motion pattern: random meandering.

This pattern is formed by sewing curve after curve after curve in every direction. The height of the curve should be equal to the width of the curve. The space between each curve should also be the same as the height of the curve.

1 Photocopy the sample on page 122. Remove the thread from your machine and stitch the paper following the lines. Do not rotate the sheet of paper as you move it across the machine bed. Notice how often you are changing directions. At first it feels like watching a beach ball bobbing in the ocean. Repeat this step as often as you feel necessary.

2 Using another practice sandwich, thread the machine and stitch out a random meandering pattern. Quilt this sandwich without using the paper on top of the fabric. Remember to focus your eyes where you are headed. Concentrate on filling in a 5" to 6" field between your hands. Maintain a moderate, steady machine speed. When one section is filled in, stop the machine, reposition your hands, and begin again.

The example on the left shows good balance. The example in the center shows good width of the curves, but the height of the curve is too exaggerated. The sample on the right shows good height and width, but obvious rows are being formed. The obvious rows come from only sewing the curves vertically and horizontally. Sewing some of the curves in a diagonal direction will make the pattern more pleasing to the eye.

Hint

After stopping to reposition the hands, many beginners find starting up again to be difficult. Stay relaxed, and start up slowly. Keep your eyes on where your last stitch is. As soon as you make the first stitch, refocus to where you are headed and build up speed. This is a separate skill that will become second nature to you with practice.

You will not achieve perfect curves all of the time; your goal is to achieve balance in pattern formation.

1

2

Once you can sew hearts in any direction, you can quilt leaves, too!

3

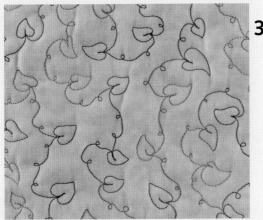

If you can quilt this, you can quilt anything. This sample was quilted using variegated thread.

Practice Exercise #4

1 Sew a heart shape in the center of a quilt sandwich. The heart shape doesn't need to be perfect, just recognizable. When you reach a complete outline of the heart shape, meander around it.

2 Once you have filled in some of the space surrounding the heart, try sewing another heart. This time, sew the heart upside down. Since we do not rotate the quilt sandwich during free-motion quilting, it is important to make shapes from any direction. Continue to fill in the space between hearts, alternating between meandering and stitching more heart shapes. Make some of the hearts point to the right and some of the hearts point to the left. As you proceed, try turning a few of the hearts into leaves.

3 Continue turning your hearts into leaves. Sew stems into the leaves, tracing your way out, then sew wavy lines to get from leaf to leaf. Add some loops among the wavy lines.

Quilting Patterns

On the following pages, many straight-line and free-motion quilting patterns are presented. Some require marking, and some patterns require no marking. Under each stitch pattern, some guidance is provided to help you decide which pattern is right for your project.

For improved visibility in the photos, I used solid-color fabrics and threads; but these patterns are suitable for all fabrics, threads and colors.

Most of the patterns are "all-over" quilting options. As you gain experience, consider using more than one quilting pattern in a single project.

Multiple quilting patterns add interest to a quilt top.

Straight-Line Quilting

Stitch-in-the-Ditch

Stitch-in-the-ditch is simply stitching directly into the seams of the quilt. By adding depth at the seam, this technique emphasizes the break from one fabric to the next. The viewer's eye is drawn to fabric prints, unusual piecing or appliqué techniques rather than to the actual quilting.

Stitch-in-the-ditch is accomplished by aligning the needle to the seams and sewing right into the seams. The stitches lay flat on the bottom fabric of the seam. Any thread can be used for stitch-in-the-ditch.

Stitch-in-the-ditch is a strong, durable application; but with so many quilting options, you don't want to limit yourself to this technique.

In this holiday example, metallic thread was used.

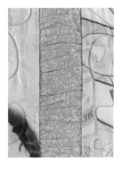

Stitch-in-the-ditch quilting adds strength to gathered fabric and emphasizes this interesting inner-border technique. (Pieced & quilted by Diana Slopic)

Stitch-in-the-Ditch

Benefits
- Requires no marking.
- Very fast for place mats and other quick projects.
- For large quilts, helps stabilize the layers until the remainder of the quilting is completed.
- Emphasizes the difference between sections or fabrics.

In this example, stitch-in-the-ditch emphasizes the "fussy-cut" novelty squares. Quilted diagonal lines push the green and pink fabric to the background.

Drawbacks
- Adds minimal texture to the quilt top.
- It can be difficult to get the needle into the "ditch."
- For intricately pieced blocks, stitch-in-the-ditch requires rotating the quilt many times.

Stitch-in-the-ditch was relatively easy on this 6" block. However, it required stopping to rotate the layers 18 times. Imagine doing that to many stars in a large project.

Parallel Diagonal Lines

Benefits

- Simplest straight-line quilting pattern.
- Easy to mark. You can use the quilt-ing guide-bar in place of marking each individual line.
- Makes a quick and easy border treatment.
- Fast for place mats and other quick projects.

Parallel diagonal lines stitched 2" apart. Because the quilting is not dense, I topstitched the decorative border to the top and eliminated the need for binding – a treatment less suitable with dense quilting.

Drawbacks

- Adds minimal texture to the quilt top.
- Possible to stitch a fold in the backing fabric if you stretch the quilt sandwich diagonally while feeding the layers into the machine.

Avoid stitching a fold into the backing by pin-basting carefully and by guiding the layers evenly into the machine with both hands.

Parallel Diagonal Lines

To quilt parallel diagonal lines you will need a 24" x 6" rotary cutting ruler and a marker. Place the 45-degree line of the ruler directly over one of the side seams connecting the border and quilt center. Larger quilts will require that you use more than one ruler; butt them together end-to-end to complete your marks.

Line up the 45-degree line to the side seam that attaches the quilt center to the border.

Hint

Be sure to place the 45-degree line of the ruler on the seam that con-nects the border and quilt top. This seam is much straighter than the outer raw edge of the border fabric.

Diagonal Squares

45-degree diagonal squares are formed by marking two sets of parallel diagonal lines. In all of the samples here, the lines were marked 2" apart.

The first set of markings uses one of the 45-degree lines of the ruler lined up on the seam that joins the border to the quilt. When marking, complete all the diagonal lines in the first direction at the same time.

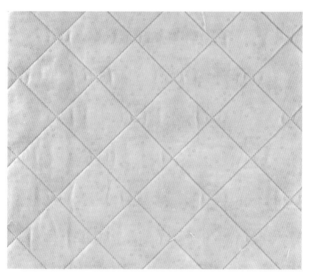

The second set of marks comes from rotating the ruler so that the other 45-degree line on the ruler is aligned with the same side seam. Complete the marks going in the opposite direction.

Diagonal Squares

Benefits
- Easy to sew.
- Results are predictable, geometric and always appropriate.
- Relatively quick if the rows are not too close together.
- Non-directional (no matter which side you view the quilt, the pattern remains the same).

Drawbacks
- All lines need to be marked for accurate results on a large project.
- Possible to stitch a fold in the backing fabric if you stretch the quilt sandwich diagonally while feeding the layers into the machine.

Hint

The distance between lines determines how dense the overall quilting will be. 2" yields good coverage and meets batting requirements for stitching density. You may sew lines closer together for the background of an appliqué project or for a border area.

First diagonal direction

Second diagonal direction

Additional Designs

Sometimes a quilt top lends itself to straight-line quilting, and the design of the quilt top makes marking lines unnecessary.
(Pieced and quilted by Phyllis Post.)

Adding a line parallel to an existing line is called "echo quilting." In this example, the second line is sewn ⅛" from each original diagonal line, creating additional texture.

A very successful treatment when using variegated threads on a marble fabric. This sample was NOT sewn with a twin needle. If you use a twin needle in this application, a zigzag stitch appears on the quilt back.

Hint

By "echo quilting," you can create additional designs while only marking one grid, especially if you use a guide bar.

Adding a second line ⅜" apart from each diagonal line creates more texture. I used the outer edge of the walking foot as my guide.

Try a third parallel line allowing ¼" between each line.

Diamonds

Diamonds are formed by completing two sets of marked lines using your ruler's 30-degree lines. Place one of the 30-degree lines directly over one of the side seams connecting the border and quilt top. In all the samples here, the lines were marked 1½" apart, yielding good coverage and meeting batting requirements for stitching density.

The first set of markings uses one of the 30-degree lines of the ruler lined up on a side seam that joins the border to the quilt. Mark all the diagonal lines in that direction.

Diamonds

Benefits
- Easy to sew.
- More interesting than the 45-degree diagonal lines.

Drawbacks
- Always needs to be marked.
- Directional (only looks good in one direction).
- 30-degree lines of the ruler can be confusing at first.

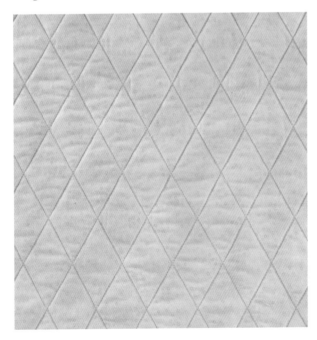

The second set of marks comes from rotating the ruler so that the opposite 30-degree line is aligned with the same side seam. Complete the marks going in the opposite direction.

Additional Designs

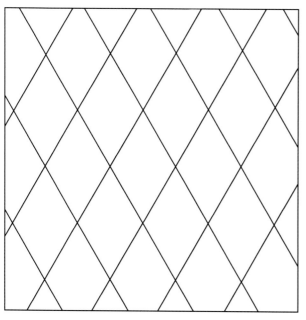

Marking Pattern

Stitch the diagonal lines as marked, then sew horizontal lines to create equilateral triangles. The horizontal lines do not need to be marked.

Sew a set of diamonds in one color, then sew the echo lines in another color. If you use the guide bar for the echo lines, you will only have to mark one set of lines.

The diagonal lines do not have to line up to the angles of a pieced block. They can be sewn on any quilt surface, and they will always look elegant.

Squares

Squares are formed by marking sets of vertical and horizontal lines that are parallel to the top and side seams of the border. In the example, the lines were marked 2" apart. This does not produce a very interesting quilt, but it is a great starting point for many other more interesting patterns.

Squares

Benefits
- Easy to sew.
- Results are predictable.
- Quick (if the rows of stitching are not too close together).
- Non-directional.

Drawbacks
- Lines need to be marked for accurate results on a large project.

Additional Designs

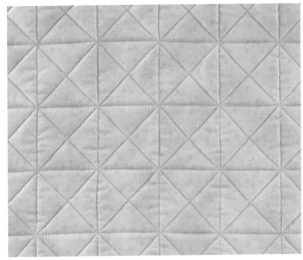

Add diagonal lines in both directions. It's a great look that is simple to sew, and you don't have to mark the diagonal lines.

Adding diagonal lines in only one direction results in an interesting dissonant look.

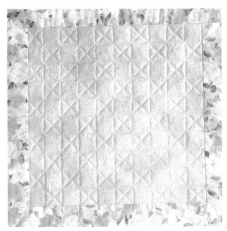

Add diagonal lines, but skip every other diagonal row. The marks were made 2" apart, but the lines were quilted 1" apart on the project by using the quilting guide bar. The diagonal lines were not marked.

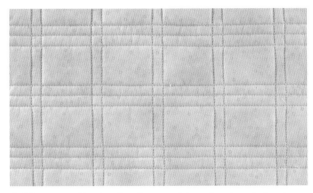

Add one vertical echo line and two horizontal echo lines to make rectangles, which look great on place mats.

Horizontal and vertical lines marked 1" apart, with quilting that looks like steps or a diagonal zigzag line.

The simple zigzag line can be used in an inner border for a fast quilting solution. Rather than mark lines on the quilt, the quilting was completed by sewing to dots I had marked at regular intervals.

This quilted star has densely quilted horizontal and vertical lines which never intersect. They force the eye to the center of the star.

Hint

If you use a guide bar to sew the echo lines, you will only have to mark the square pattern once.

Echo Quilting

Echo quilting occurs when a line is sewn parallel to a quilting line, a seam line or a fabric motif.

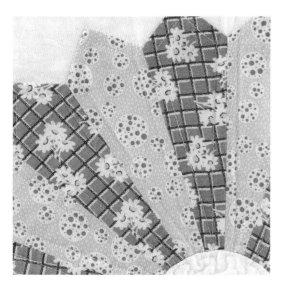

Benefits
• Requires no marking.
• Predictable results.
• Non-directional.

Drawbacks
• Sometimes requires rotating the quilt.
• Cumbersome on a large quilt.

Special Designs

As long as you are willing to mark, sew and rotate, any straight-line design can be quilted with a walking foot. Keep in mind rotating the quilt requires stopping with the needle down, lifting the presser foot, rotating the quilt, putting the presser foot back down and continuing to sew to the next turn.

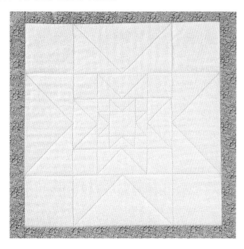

Benefits
• Beautiful to look at.
• Interesting and recognizable.

Drawbacks
• Almost always requires that the quilt sandwich be rotated many times.
• Requires advanced planning and marking.
• Cumbersome on a large project.

Unmarked Free-Motion Quilting

The free-motion section is broken into two parts. The first part shows all-over quilting patterns that do not require marking. The second part shows free-motion patterns that require at least some marking. On pages 122-125, you will find drawings of the basic unmarked all-over designs. For practice, photocopy the drawings, and "sew" them without thread.

None of the quilting patterns require an artistic background. They are simple lines that anyone can complete. Stencils are available for more refined quilting options at your quilt shop.

Stitch-in-the-Ditch

Many novice quilters believe stitch-in-the-ditch is only a straight-line quilting technique, but it is often used to quilt around an appliqué design to provide stability to the quilt layers without showing visible stitches around the appliqué.

Stitch-in-the-ditch is accomplished by sewing right into the seams. The stitches lay flat on the background fabric. Any thread can be used for stitch-in-the-ditch.

Stitch-in-the-Ditch

Benefits
- Requires no marking.
- Helps to puff out an appliqué design.

Drawbacks
- Adds minimal texture.
- Difficult to get the needle into the "ditch."

The umbrella and duckie were stitched all the way around their edges to meet batting requirements. The raindrop fabric looked beautiful without quilting lines, so other quilting options were not desirable.

Random Meandering

Benefits

- Easy to sew.
- Used in a background, it forces the background to the back.
- Adds texture without taking center stage.
- Versatile and graceful.
- Non-directional.

Drawbacks

- Can get used too often.
- Difficult to maintain consistent stitches.

By meandering in the background, the stems and leaves of this quilt pop forward.

Random Meandering

Random meandering is one of the most versatile stitch patterns for free-motion quilting enthusiasts. It adds texture without distraction, and it can be sewn in any size. See page 122 for a practice sheet.

Hint

When random meandering, novice quilters tend to speed up the pace the quilt layers are moved over the sewing bed. But they fail to speed up the rate of the machine, creating very large or inconsistent stitches, especially when the pattern is large. Be sure you keep a steady rhythm.

Tiny meandering is known as stippling. This is a very time-consuming application.

In the example above, the border fabric was quilted in the background using a variegated yellow thread. The flowers, leaves and butterflies stand out, even at a great distance. Compare this to the same fabric quilted all over with a solid cream-colored thread to the right. It is pretty, but the design of the fabric is not as dramatic.

Loops

Loops create a whimsical look on a textured quilt surface. They are formed by combining graceful, wavy lines and loops. The paper practice sheet for loops is on page 123.

Loops

Benefits
- Ideal in a juvenile novelty print.
- Fast to quilt.
- Great with variegated threads.
- Good for connecting other designs, such as leaves and flowers.

Drawbacks
- Difficult to use in tight spaces.
- Difficult to keep random.

Hint

To keep a random look to your loops, try alternating between clockwise and counterclockwise formations.

In this example, loops join the leaves of a vine in a narrow 1" inner border.

Flames

Flames

Benefits
- Add excitement to the quilt surface.
- Look great with metallic thread.

Drawbacks
- Highly recognizable.
- Won't work with some fabric themes, such as a 1930's reproduction quilt.
- Difficult to maintain consistent spacing and random appearance.
- Thread tension can be poor at the tip of the flame.
- If stitched vertically, flames are highly directional.

Flames are formed with wavy snake lines and sharp points. It takes a little getting used to, but if you work with the practice pattern on page 123, you will get the hang of it.

Hint

If your tension becomes poor at the top of the pattern, stop the needle at the tip of the point, and then continue sewing. You only need to stop for a moment. A momentary pause at sharp points can make a big difference.

Flames give this color wheel dimension, help tie all of the colors together, and fit beautifully with the "sharp" points of the paper-pieced medallion.

Flames do not need to be directional.

Landscape Texture

Landscape texture is formed by making long horizontal lines, small curves, and short vertical lines. It has the effect of looking like water, snow or clouds. There is no diagonal movement.

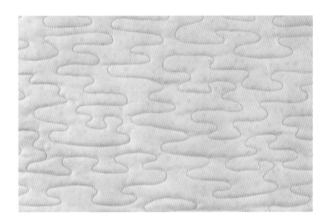

Landscape Texture

Benefits
- Effective in a landscape quilt.
- Good for borders on a busy print.
- Adds more texture than random meandering.

Drawbacks
- Not suitable on solid-colored fabrics (unless you're quilting water on a landscape quilt).
- Challenging to maintain random pattern.

Hint

Use the practice tracing on page 124 to get used to the random motion of the landscape texture pattern.

Used vertically with variegated thread, landscape texture also makes great bark texture for a tree.

Create snow on a pine tree with long, diagonal lines, some vertical stitching and little horizontal movement.

Swirls and Curls

Benefits
- Non-directional.
- Creates an unexpected texture when used as an all-over design.
- Crescent points are good for a tight corner.

Drawbacks
- Not a strong geometric texture.
- Thread tension can be poor at the tip of the crescent.

Swirls and Curls

This elegant pattern is formed with wavy lines, curvy lines, and crescents. The crescents are used to echo the curls. The paper practice sheet for swirls and curls is on page 124.

Hint

If your tension becomes poor at the tip of the pattern, stop the needle at the tip of the crescent, and then continue sewing. You only need to stop for a moment. A momentary pause at sharp points can make a big difference.

Swirls and curls stitched on a marbled fabric using variegated blue thread.

Busy Asian prints are enhanced with swirls and curls using a forest-green metallic thread.

Benefits
- Versatile.
- Similar to random meandering, but all the lines are straight.

Drawbacks
- Too angular to be considered graceful.
- Keeping the lines straight can be a challenge.

Try-Angles

Try-angles are strong and angular and look great on novelty prints. They are formed using only points and straight lines. Try-angles are free-motion patterns, they do not lend themselves to straight-line quilting because of the amount of angles and corners. Practice on paper by photocopying the pattern on page 125.

Hint

To help keep your quilting lines straight, be sure to warm up for a few minutes before applying the stitches to your quilt.

Try layering the quilting lines with a variety of cotton and metallic threads.

Unmarked Free-Motion Quilting Combinations

Some all-over designs combine more than one motif for a more interesting look, like leaves with loops. The following examples combine additional motifs.

Teardrops

Circles and teardrops are very versatile. The example at right uses teardrops as the basis for the pattern. The circles are combined with echo quilting. The echo quilting lines enable you to get from one place to the next in the quilt to fill in the areas. It can be stitched out in all sizes.

Hint

Teardrops and circles make a lovely inner-border treatment.

Pachysandra

Pachysandra is formed by combining echo teardrops, flower petal leaves and echo quilting. The small flower center and the echo quilting are dense stitching lines quilted among large, puffy flower petals. The contrast between dense stitching and puffy leaves adds wonderful texture to a quilt surface.

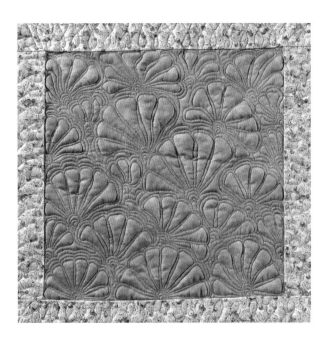

Leaves and Flowers

There are many leaves and flowers in nature. In quilting, there are even more, ranging from realistic to whimsical. Combining them with stems, wavy lines and loops, the possibilities are endless!

In this border, the leaves point to the sides and center of the quilt since the stems emerge from the outside edge of the border.

Leaves combined with a very simple flower for a quick border treatment.

Easy Border Solutions

Almost all quilting patterns are suitable for borders. However, some quilts have inner borders or narrow outer borders which require a fast and simple solution. Give one of the following unmarked options a try.

This heart pattern is actually sewn in four separate lines. Quilt the blue line (right side of heart) first, all the way around the quilt. When you get back to the beginning, stitch the red line (left side of the heart). For added texture, add echo quilting: Stitch the green line, then stitch the brown line.

START HERE

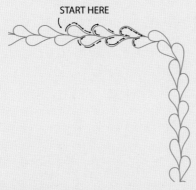

The vine is sewn almost like the hearts, except you are sewing a single line, closing the leaf up against the stem. The arrows indicate stitching direction.

This is simple back-and-forth looping. Plan ahead for the corners by marking them to keep yourself from getting lost.

Marked Free-Motion Quilting

In this example, black thread was used on all the large flowers, butterflies and leaves. Random meandering was used in the background. The black thread and puff from the batting makes the flowers and leaves stand out more when viewed from a distance.

Tracing and Pre-Printed Panels

Preprinted fabric panels can be quilted using any one of the previous straight-line or free-motion panels. Another option is to trace over the larger design elements of the fabric.

To enable the butterflies to stand out, they were traced with a bright colored thread.

Vines

While vines can be easily quilted without any marking lines, it may give you more confidence in the beginning to mark all or part of the design.

Mark this.

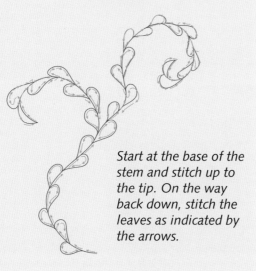

Start at the base of the stem and stitch up to the tip. On the way back down, stitch the leaves as indicated by the arrows.

Vines can be used to fill in start points.

Mark just the stems to make sure you have balanced coverage. Then start stitching in the center and travel up each stem; and on the way back down, add the leaves of the vine.

Stencils

Hundreds of stencils are available today that can enhance a quilt surface. Because of the popularity of free-motion quilting, many stencils are produced in the form of continuous line designs. Some stencils come with a label that indicates the direction the design should be stitched.

Additional simple designs and new, intricate designs are available in books specifically for tracing onto paper. After the design has been traced onto the paper, it is pinned to the quilt surface. The quilter sews over the paper, tracing the designs. The tracing paper is then torn away. Any theme fabric has a counterpart somewhere in a stencil.

Another option is to trace a favorite design onto lightweight interfacing. Trace and cut many designs. Then spray the back with a temporary fabric adhesive. Place the cut-outs in a uniform or random arrangement onto the quilt surface. Quilt around each image. Random meandering or stippling can be filled in between each image.

A marked free-motion design using a heart-shaped cookie cutter as a stencil.

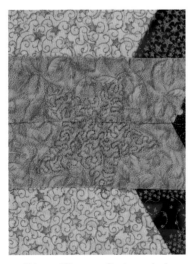

The stars on this quilt were first made by quilting around star-shaped, lightweight-interfacing stencils. The stencils were then removed, and the inside of each star was stippled.

This feather design was made with a traced stencil. Stippling was then added in the center and around the outside.

Another continuous line treatment is to combine free-motion straight lines with recognizable images. I like to use cookie cutters for this application. To use this technique, mark the quilt with a grid of horizontal and vertical lines so that the tracings of the cookie cutter can be spaced evenly.

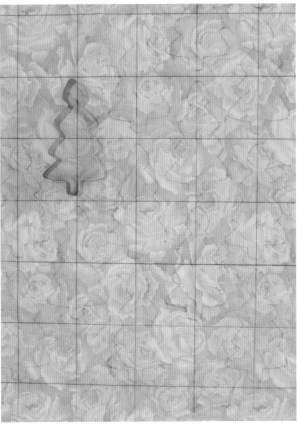

The horizontal lines will not be quilted. Only the vertical lines and the images are quilted.

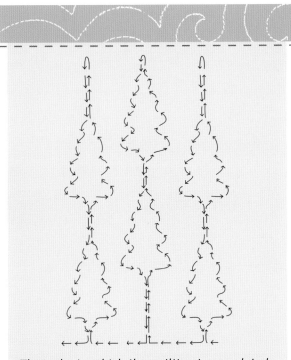

The order in which the quilting is completed is indicated by the arrows.

Wavy Lines

Any straight-line pattern can be stitched using free-motion wavy lines. The only real challenge is to maintain your rhythm when quilting the long lines.

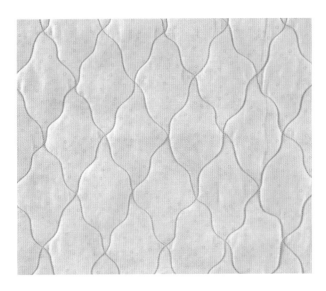

Clamshells

Clamshells in any size are a beautiful quilting treatment, but they do require marking. To maintain a balanced framework, it is a good idea to draw a grid (horizontal and vertical lines) and then mark the individual clamshells with a stencil. Some clamshell stencils let you mark repeated clamshells without a grid.

In this example, the single line clamshells were marked. But echo quilting was added in two of the corners. In the opposite two corners, an additional loop was added. The quilting directions are illustrated here:

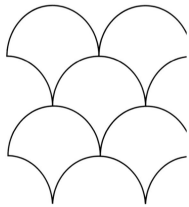

In all of the clamshell examples, this simple grid was marked using a 1" circle template.

The red line represents the first line of quilting. It is sewn from left to right. At the end of the row, change directions. The echo quilting, represented by the blue line, is sewn from right to left.

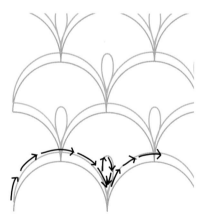

The additional loop embellishment is stitched during the first line of quilting. The red line represents the first line of quilting. It is sewn from left to right. At the end of the row, change directions. The echo quilting, represented by the blue line, is sewn from right to left. The arrows indicate the direction of stitching to form the loops.

Quilting Individual Blocks

Any repeated block of a quilt, such as stars or nine-patch blocks, can be quilted one at a time as individual blocks. You can use a stencil or a single image that you can sew without markings.

Any free-motion design can be re-sized for any block.

In this illustration, the flower was enlarged to fill up a nine-patch block.

There are many ways to quilt individual star blocks.

Echo quilting does not always mean quilting a parallel line. This wavy-line echo quilting brightens the star.

The quilted star in the center of this block was formed by gluing two 1¼" offset squares of paper together. Only the outline of the paper star was marked in the center of the star. The flowing lines are stitched out from the points of the center star.

Putting It All Together

Your quilt top is finished, the backing fabric is pieced, and your batting is off to the side, laying over a chair. Now what? There is nothing more frustrating to a novice quilter than staring at a completed quilt top and wondering, "How am I going to quilt this?"

Before selecting a quilting pattern, there are several questions you may wish to consider regarding technical aspects and artistic aspects of the quilt.

Technical Considerations

Where is this quilt going to go when it is finished?

A project that is meant to hang on a wall will not need as much quilting to maintain its structural integrity over time. Therefore, light quilting is an option, and all threads can be used for the quilting.

A quilt that will be heavily used and laundered needs to be strong and durable, so it shouldn't use metallic or rayon threads. Choose a quilting pattern that will hold up to repeated launderings.

What are the quilting recommendations for the batting you plan to use?

Batting recommendations for quilting and laundering are not to be taken lightly. Manufacturers want consumers to be happy with their product. Research has determined the best quilting recommendations, and you are wise not to take any chances by "stretching the limit."

Do you mind taking the time to mark your quilt?

Some quilting patterns require that you pre-mark the quilt top before basting the layers together. This is especially true of many straight-line patterns and plastic stencils. Free-motion quilting has gained popularity among those who do not have the patience or interest in the marking step.

What are your skills?

I do not believe you become a proficient quilter by practicing only on muslin sandwiches. There is a time and place for such practice; it helps determine thread tension, and it's helpful for warming up. Practice sandwiches are a good way to work out a new quilting pattern.

However, the only way to get better at quilting is to make an actual quilt. Here's an opportunity to use up your scraps by making simple lap quilts or place mats. When making these simple projects, think about using a quilting pattern that is new to you, but not too difficult. You want to stretch your skills a little bit at a time.

My first attempt at random meandering on a quilt. When I hang this quilt in November, I am reminded of how far I have come as a quilter.

If you are just starting out, consider an easy quilting idea. This project was completed by sewing individual stars and swirls using various colors of rayon thread. The stars and swirls were placed randomly on the quilt surface.

What equipment do you have?

Quilting a bed-sized quilt in a cramped space is an unrealistic idea. Is your sewing machine in excellent working order, and do you know how to use it? If you are learning how to sew for the first time, keep it simple. It takes time to know your sewing machine intimately. Also, a well-lit quilting area is essential to prevent eye strain. Use lighting that reduces glare.

How much time do you have to finish this quilt?

If this quilt is for your soon-to-be daughter-in-law, and the wedding is next weekend, keep it simple. If you do not have much time to complete a project, select a quilting design that can be finished quickly, and avoid specialty threads that may be tricky to use.

Is the way a quilt drapes important to you?

Good quilts lay flat on a wall, table or bed. If a quilt does not lay flat, the cause is either poor piecing or unbalanced quilting. Quilting shrinks a quilt. The more stitching, the more the quilt will shrink. When choosing how to complete a quilt, keep in mind that the entire surface must be quilted uniformly, even if more than one pattern was used on a quilt. It is not a good idea to have one section of a quilt densely quilted and another part lightly quilted. Unless I am using one pattern over the entire quilt surface, I rarely decide on a border treatment until the center of the quilt is completed. This way I can see how dense my quilting needs to be on the border in order to make the quilt lay flat.

Artistic Considerations

What kind of thread will enhance the feeling of this quilt?

Thread weight, fiber content and color all make a difference in the finished project. Quilting can help to blend seemingly unrelated fabrics. Thread color and fiber content can help enhance the quilt. Would you like to use a single colored thread or more than one color?

For this quilt, I quilted a spider web pattern with alternating black and orange thread. On the darkest fabrics, the black lines disappear, and only the orange lines are obvious. On the orange fabric, the orange thread disappears while the black lines prevail. Simple thread color changes can make a world of difference.

Though the fabrics are related by theme, the colors are not matched. The sample on top is unquilted. On the bottom, the quilting lines help to blend the fabrics.

How much texture do you want?

By texture, I am referring to the relationship between the quilted areas and the unquilted areas. If the stitched lines are very close together, the surface of the quilt is flat. Combinations of stippling and feathered motifs are beautiful because there is contrast between the centers of the feathering and the stippling. Batting and quilting used together create the texture. Do you want the quilting to emphasize pieced elements or to blend the pieced fabrics together? Decide if you want the quilting to take center stage or to remain in the background so that the piecing or appliqué takes center stage.

How do you want to quilt a top when all of the blocks are different?

If you have completed a block-of-the-month quilt where every block is a different design, quilting helps to bring a unifying quality to the separate blocks. Block-of-the-month quilts also look great with an all-over straight-line or free-motion pattern. Avoid stitch-in-the-ditch on these quilts. They are charming in their simplicity, and deserve more consideration for quilting.

Did you use cotton batting, and are you going to wash it and then use heat in your dryer?

Notice that I did not ask this question in the technical section. I know this is not a recommended treatment by batting manufacturers. But it is hard to resist shrinking that batting to obtain an instant antique look for those quilt tops which use 1930s or Civil War era fabrics and patterns!

This feathered pillow top has been washed and dried many times. I love the texture. Not surprisingly, so do my dogs!

Does your quilt have any appliqué designs?

Choose an all-over quilting design that moves the background fabric to the visual back in order to emphasize the appliqué. You can also quilt over the appliqué lines to blend the appliqué into the background.

With the background quilted, the batting pushes the appliquéd sunflowers to the surface, even though the appliqué petals have been quilted in the center.

This block has stitch-in-the-ditch quilting only. If this is the only quilting used, the sashing will need to be lightly quilted.

Does your quilt incorporate any embroidery designs?

Placing embroidery designs into quilts is a wonderful way to enjoy the vast array of home embroidery motifs. They take special consideration, since quilting through an embroidery design is not desirable. You can quilt the fabric around the embroidery design, or you can stitch-in-the-ditch around the outside of the embroidered block. Depending on the background fabric, the quilting will either enhance or detract from the design.

This example shows an embroidery design with a single line of echo quilting. It is a simple finish.

This example has random meandering around the entire design. It makes the embroidery stand out. While a great treatment, the sashings will need similar quilting to enable the wall hanging to lay flat.

This example has 45-degree, straight-line quilting. The lines are spaced 1½" apart, except where the embroidery design is placed. It doesn't matter that the lines are not evenly spaced throughout, as long as the spacing is uniformly applied over the entire quilt surface.

How do you want to fill in the spaces of your quilt?

Quilting breathes life into an otherwise flat surface. In some ways, it is much like coloring in a coloring book. You can complete an all-over design or fill in the spaces with colored thread. If the question "How should I quilt this?" is too intimidating for you, try asking yourself "How do I want to fill in the spaces?"

Pleasing yourself should be the primary consideration when choosing a quilting pattern. Each project, no matter how small, will make you a better quilter. Do not rip out stitches if they are less than perfect. Most of the time, individual stitches cannot be seen. Errors are not usually noticeable to others. Remember that quilting is not the art of perfection. It is simply doing something you love. If you find an error on the back of the quilt that is not present on the front of the quilt, don't worry about it. We learn from our mistakes.

If you find an error on the back of a quilt that bothers you, place a label over it. This is much faster than ripping out stitches!

Photocopy and complete this work sheet when you are planning your project. At the conclusion of the project, make notes about what worked well and what did not work. Record how long it took you to complete the quilt. File the completed work sheet as a reference for future projects.

Quilt Work Sheet

Technical Considerations:

1. Where is this quilt going to go when it is finished?

   This quilt is:
   ___ a wall hanging
   ___ a bed quilt

   This quilt will:
   ___ not be used heavily
   ___ will be used heavily and laundered frequently

   What is the size of the quilt?_____

2. What are the quilting recommendations for the batting you plan to use?

   Fiber content of the batting: _____
   Manufacturer's recommendation for quilt line density: _____ inches apart

3. Am I going to mark my quilt?

   _____ yes _____ no

4. What are my skills?

   Straight-line: ___ Novice
   ___ Limited experience ___ Intermediate
   Free-motion: ___ Novice
   ___ Limited experience ___ Intermediate

5. What kind of equipment and quilting space do I have?

   ___ Space is limited and cramped
   ___ Space is satisfactory for the size of the project
   ___ Sewing machine and related notions are not satisfactory for a large project
   ___ Sewing machine and related notions are satisfactory for a large project

6. How much time do I have to finish this quilt?

   Projected completion date: _____

7. Is the way a quilt drapes important? What is my plan for balanced quilting density throughout the entire project?

Artistic Considerations:

1. What kind of thread will enhance the feeling of this quilt?

   Fiber content of the thread: _____
   Thread weight: _____

2. How much texture do I want?

3. How do I want to quilt a top where all of the blocks are different?

4. Did I use cotton or wool batting, and am I going to wash it and then use heat in the dryer?

5. Does my quilt have any appliqué?

6. Does my quilt incorporate embroidery designs or fussy cut fabrics?

7. How do I want to fill the spaces of my quilt?

NOTES:

Projects

We all know that practice makes perfect. However, eventually it is time to walk away from the practice sandwiches and apply your skills to actual projects. The six simple projects included here have been chosen to help you build your skill level.

Materials for All Projects

Sewing machine
Scissors to clip thread
Scissors to cut fabric
Extension table
    (necessary for all free-motion quilting)
Seam ripper
Marking pencil
Ironing board and iron
Walking foot or free-motion foot
Free Motion Slider (optional)
    for all free-motion quilting
Sewing machine needles appropriate
    for piecing and quilting
Straight pins
Basting safety pins
Single needle plate
Lint brush
Gripping gloves or hoop
Serger Tweezers
    (Optional. Use to grab loose threads
    off the quilt)
Rotary cutter and mat
24" x 6" ruler
Digital camera
    (Optional. Use to maintain a photo
    journal of your work)

Pillow and Tissue-Box Cover

By framing the 10" square with a treasured novelty print, and turning it into a pillow cover, you have a ready-made gift for any occasion. If you wish to see your practice stitches get "lost" in the fabric, use a busy print for the center.

Only the front of the pillow is quilted. The back of the pillow uses two overlapping fabric panels, known as an envelope closure. Because the panels overlap by approximately 6", there is no need for hook-and-loop tape or zippers. The pillow form slides in and out of the envelope closure, making it easy to launder.

This pillow cover will help you:

- Improve either straight-line quilting or free-motion quilting.
- Test quilting patterns before using them in a larger quilt. The majority of the quilting is done inside the 10" center square. If you find you do not enjoy quilting a pattern inside a 10" square, you won't be happy quilting it in a larger project.
- Test new threads and ideas. You can quilt only the center, or you can quilt the center and border.
- Practice the stitch-in-the-ditch technique.

Finished size: 14" square before quilting

Materials

Sewing machine and accessories from
    page 81
Neutral thread for piecing
Quilting thread
14" pillow form

Fabric

½ yd. novelty print for pillow-top border
    and envelope-style back panels
10½" square piece of fabric for pillow
    center
17" x 17" piece of muslin
16" x 16" piece of batting

Cutting Directions

From the ½ yd. print, cut:

- one 2½" wide strip. From this strip,
  cut two pieces 14½" long for the top
  and bottom borders.

- one 10½" wide strip. From this strip,
  cut two 10½" x 2½" strips along the
  grain of the fabric for the side borders.

- two 10½" x 14½" panels for the
  envelope-style pillow back.

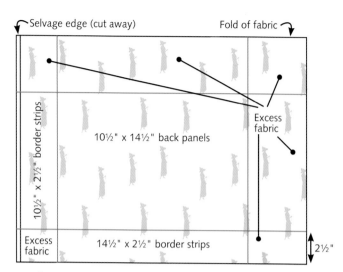

*When using directional fabric, fold the fabric and cut
as shown.*

1 Using a ¼" seam, sew the 2½" x 10½"
strips to the sides of the pillow center. Press
seams towards the border strips. Using a ¼"
seam, sew the 2½" x 14½" strips to the two
remaining sides. Press seams to the border
strips.

*Make sure to face all of the directional prints of the
border fabric in the same direction.*

2 Mark the center square if the quilting pattern
you wish to use requires marking.

In the completed sample, I added a single line of echo quilting around the outside of the stencil design after the motif was quilted.

3 Make your quilt sandwich using the 17" muslin square for the backing. Prepare your quilt sandwich according to the directions that start on page 23.

4 Using the "stitch-in-the-ditch" straight-line machine quilting technique, stitch in the seams where the border is attached to the center square.

5 Complete the quilting using straight-line or free-motion quilting techniques.

6 Square up the completed pillow top to approximately 14½" square, cutting away the excess batting and backing.

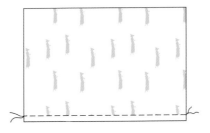

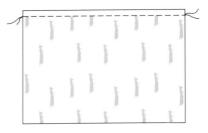

Because the example uses a directional fabric, it is necessary to complete Step 7 at the top edge of one panel, and the bottom edge of the other panel as shown.

7 On each back panel, double fold one long edge ¼" and sew in place. This will finish the exposed edges.

8 With right sides together, place the back panels on the pillow top, lining up the sides, and overlapping the finished edges of the back panels. Place the top panel down first, then the bottom panel. Pin in place. Sew a ¼" seam around the entire outside edge. Continue to pay attention to which way the panels face if using a directional novelty print.

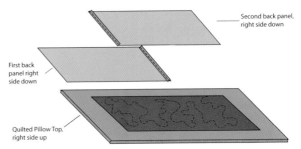

Layer the pillow-back panels as shown, pin in place and sew with a ¼" seam.

9 In order to reduce fray, secure the outside edges with a zigzag or overlock stitch. You'll find that these soft pillows will be heavily used.

10 Turn the pillow inside out through the back-panel opening, and insert the 14" pillow form.

Tissue-Box Cover

All quilters love quick projects to give away. To turn this pillow top into a "Thinking-of-You" or "Get-Well" treat for someone special, purchase an extra fat quarter of the novelty print, and make a Tissue-Box Cover sized for the 4½" cubed boxes of tissues. The only other materials you need are 28" of coordinating ribbon and a 6" square-up ruler. Yardage for the pillow cover and the tissue-box cover together is ⅞ yd. From this yardage, you will have enough fabric for two tissue-box covers and one pillow cover.

1 Trim a fat quarter into a 20" x 15" panel, and zigzag stitch along the 20" edge.

2 Sew a ½" or 14 mm button hole centered 2⅞" down from the top edge. Cut button hole open.

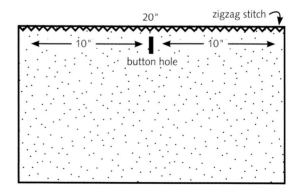

3 Fold the bag so the right sides are together. Sew a ½" seam connecting the two 15" sides. Then stitch the bottom edge using a ½" seam.

4 With right sides together, align the bag so that the 15" side seam lies directly behind the button hole. Smooth the bottom corners out so that a square is formed at the bottom when laid flat on a table.

5 Aligning your 6" square-up ruler, mark a line exactly 4½" long from edge to edge along the lower corner. The marked line is perpendicular to the button hole and the sides of the bag. Stitch a seam on the marked line. Trim the excess corner fabric, leaving a ¼" seam allowance. Repeat this step on the opposite corner making sure to turn the bag over and folding the bag up and out of your way.

6 Turn the bag right side out. Fold the top edge over 2" with wrong sides together. Sew two lines parallel all the way around the top edge on either side of the button-hole opening.

7 Thread coordinating ribbon through the buttonhole. Place the tissue box inside the bag, and pull up the first tissue. Loosely tie the bag closed around the tissue.

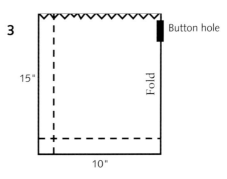

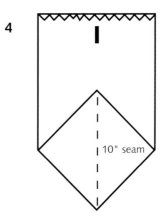

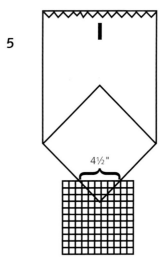

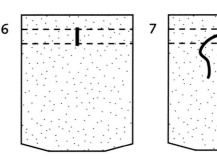

Rag Quilt

This project is designed with one goal in mind: Each of the finished 8" squares are quilted BEFORE they are pieced together. Because of this unusual construction technique, these squares are easy to use for practicing free-motion quilting. Since the project uses flannel prints for the blocks, and a single layer of flannel in place of batting, no pin-basting is needed. The best part is that the nap of the flannel fabric hides all stitch imperfections.

The sample shown was made when I had purchased a new sewing machine. I wanted an easy project to become familiar with my new machine. After sewing over 100 squares, I was more than proficient using my new machine

for free-motion quilting. The squares start off in their raw form as 9" squares, but you only need to fill a 7" square area with quilting. A 9" square is a manageable block for any quilter.

Choose whatever finished project size you wish. Yardage requirements are provided in six sizes. It is easily altered to suit any size needed. To maintain a scrappy appearance, only ½ yd. of each flannel fabric was used, providing enough fabric for four completed squares. DO NOT pre-wash the colored flannel. DO pre-wash the flannel batting. By washing the inside fabric, but not the outside fabric, you will create additional texture when the completed project is laundered.

RAG QUILT Yardage Chart

Finished Size of Quilt	Total number of squares in completed project	Total number of half yard cuts of colored flannel fabrics for scrappy look	Cutting the outside flannel squares *(Do not pre-wash this fabric)*	Amount of white flannel for batting *(Do pre-wash and machine dry this flannel used as batting)*
Crib Quilt 40" x 56"	5 squares across 7 squares down 35 total squares	four ½ yard cuts totaling 2 yards	Cut each ½ yard length of fabric into four pairs of 9" squares. Cut 35 pairs of 9" squares.	1⅔ yards — cut seven 8" strips. From each strip, cut five 8" squares.
Lap Quilt 56" x 80"	7 squares across 10 squares down 70 total squares	eighteen ½ yard cuts totaling 9 yards	Cut each ½ yard length of fabric into four pairs of 9" squares. Cut 70 pairs of 9" squares.	3¼ yards — cut fourteen 8" strips. From each strip, cut five 8" squares.
Twin Quilt 72" x 104"	9 squares across 13 squares down 117 total squares	thirty ½ yard cuts totaling 15 yards	Cut each ½ yard length of fabric into four pairs of 9" squares. Cut 117 pairs of 9" squares.	5⅔ yards — cut twenty-four 8" strips. From each strip, cut five 8" squares.
Full Quilt 88" x 112"	11 squares across 14 squares down 154 total squares	thirty-nine ½ yard cuts totaling 19½ yards	Cut each ½ yard length of fabric into four pairs of 9" squares. Cut 154 pairs of 9" squares.	7⅔ yards — cut thirty-one 8" strips. From each strip, cut five 8" squares.
Queen Quilt 96" x 112"	12 squares across 14 squares down 168 total squares	forty-two ½ yard cuts totaling 21 yards	Cut each ½ yard length of fabric into four pairs of 9" squares. Cut 168 pairs of 9" squares.	8⅓ yards — cut thirty-four 8" strips. From each strip, cut five 8" squares.
King Quilt 104" x 120"	13 squares across 15 squares down 195 total squares	forty-nine ½ yard cuts totaling 24½ yards	Cut each ½ yard length of fabric into four pairs of 9" squares. Cut 195 pairs of 9" squares.	10 yards — cut thirty-nine 8" strips. From each strip, cut five 8" squares.

Materials

Sewing machine and accessories from page 81

Neutral thread for piecing

Coordinating quilting thread

1 Sandwich one 8" piece of white flannel between two 9" squares of the print flannel. The white square is centered inside the 9" squares as shown.

2 Quilt the 9" flannel sandwich. Center the quilting so that there is approximately 1" of unquilted space on all four sides. I used random meandering in every square of the sample with 100% cotton, solid-colored coordinating thread. However, you should quilt your project using any quilting pattern. The more variety, the more proficient in free-motion quilting you will become.

3 Repeat Steps 1 and 2 until all the 9" squares are quilted.

4 Arrange your squares using the yardage chart to determine the number of rows and columns.

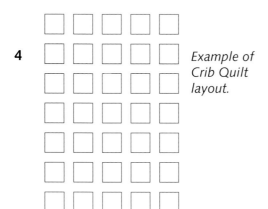

Example of Crib Quilt layout.

1

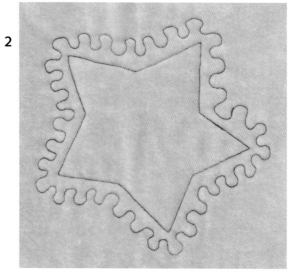

With the wrong side of a 9" flannel-fabric square faced up, place an 8" square of white flannel fabric on top. Over this, place the second colored flannel over the white square, wrong sides together. The right sides of the colored flannel fabric should be facing out.

2

In this example, the 9" square was marked with a five-point star. A curvy line of echo quilting was added around the star for additional interest. Contrasting thread was used for the purpose of photography.

5 Once the squares have been arranged, begin joining them into rows. To join squares, place them right sides together and sew using a ½" seam allowance. Sew together one row at a time. You do not need to press any seams.

6 Starting at the top, join the first two rows using a ½" seam allowance. As you come to intersecting seams, open each seam, and continue to sew the two rows together.

7 Add each row one at a time until all the rows have been attached.

8 Once all the rows have been sewn, snip the seam allowance fabric. The snips should be made every ¼" to ½".

Hint

Be sure not to accidentally snip the stitching at the seam. This step can be tiring, so work on a small section every day until the entire quilt is snipped.

9 Launder the quilt. I laundered the completed sample at a commercial laundromat because of the extra large washing machines and dryers.

The more wear and laundering the quilt receives, the more the edges will fray evenly for a soft, textured finish. Both sides of this quilt are the right side!

Hint

Because of the heavy nature of the flannel fabrics, it is best to use a sturdy, size 90 topstitch needle for piecing together the 9" squares.

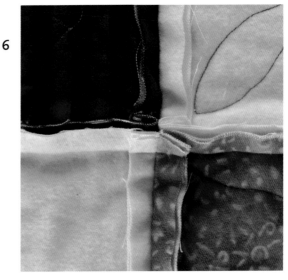

6

By opening the seams at each intersection where four blocks come together, you are spreading out the bulk.

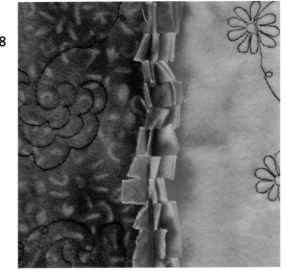

8

Snip the raw edges every ¼" to ½".

Sweet Hearts

This small wall hanging will help you:

• See how the quilting enhances and puffs up appliqué, since only the background and border are quilted.

• Learn to quilt with dark thread on a dark background fabric, which is a challenge and requires additional lighting.

• Plan ahead so you quilt around the hearts in one continuous line.

Finished size: 12½" x 12½" before quilting

Materials

Sewing machine and accessories from
    page 81
Neutral thread used for piecing
Black thread for the appliqué
Quilting thread
4½" x 15" square piece of fusible web
14" square piece of batting

Fabric

1 fat quarter of a light-colored, small-
    floral print for the hearts and the
    backing
1 fat quarter of dark fabric for the
    background and binding
1 fat quarter for the border

Cutting Directions

From the light-colored, small-floral print,
cut:

• one 5" x 18" strip away from the
    raw-edge end. Square the remaining
    section to 14" square and set aside for
    the backing

From the dark fabric, cut:

• four 1⅜" strips for the binding

• one 9½" square for the background

From the fat quarter for the border, cut:

• two 2" x 9½" strips on the cross grain

• two 2" x 12½" strips on the cross
    grain

1 Trace the hearts found on page 120 onto the paper part of the fusible web. Trace one of the 1st heart; trace one of the 2nd heart; trace three of the 3rd heart; trace two of the 4th heart; trace two of the 5th heart; trace three of the 6th heart; trace four of the 7th heart.

2 Following the manufacturer's directions, press the marked fusible web to the wrong side of the 5" x 18" heart fabric.

3 Cut out the hearts, and remove the paper backing. At the ironing board, arrange the hearts on the right side of the 9½" background square, leaving at least ½" all the way around the outer edge of the background fabric. When the hearts are arranged, fuse the hearts to the background fabric using a medium temperature iron without steam.

3

It is easiest to move the small hearts with a long tweezers.

4 Set your sewing machine to a small-sized blanket stitch (if you do not have this stitch, use a zigzag stitch). Sew around each heart to secure them to the background fabric.

5 Using a ¼" seam allowance, sew the two 9½" long border strips to each side and press out. Then attach the two 12½" border strips to the top and bottom. Press out.

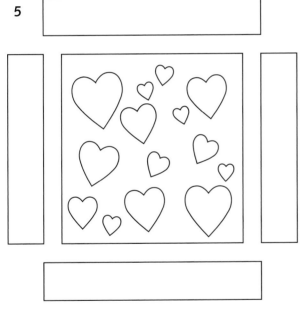

Start with the two side-border strips, and then add the top and bottom border strips.

6 Layer the quilt sandwich according to the directions on page 23. Set up your sewing machine for free-motion quilting. Add additional lighting to your work area, and meander around every heart using dark-colored thread. Pay careful attention as you quilt around every heart, so you don't get lost or quilt yourself into a dead end. Additional lighting helps with this step.

7 Quilt the border with coordinating thread. Trim away excess batting and backing. Attach the single-layer binding according to the directions on page 117.

Americana Place Mats

This project, comprised of four placements, will help you:

- Learn to save time by planning ahead. The four place mats can be quickly pin basted at one time on a single piece of backing and a single piece of batting.

- Incorporate both straight-line and free-motion patterns.

- Learn to balance straight-line and free-motion quilting for uniform quilt density.

Hint

It takes a little experimentation to know how dense the free-motion quilting needs to be in comparison to the straight-line quilting. Different sewing machines will produce different results. Uniform density is important for the place mats to lay flat.

Finished size: 14" x 20" before quilting

Materials (for Four Place Mats)

Sewing machine and accessories from
    page 81
Neutral thread used for piecing
Red and navy blue thread for the
    appliqué
Quilting thread
6½" square of fusible web for the stars
    of the flag
6½" x 17" piece of fusible web for the
    red stripes of the flag
35" x 40" piece of batting

Fabric (for Four Place Mats)

1 yd. or four fat quarters of a novelty flag
    fabric or other favorite red, white and
    blue fabric
1 yd. of a novelty-print fabric for the
    backing
½ yd. of white fabric for the background
    behind the flag
½ yd. of red fabric for the binding and
    the flag stripes
7" square of navy blue fabric with tiny
    white stars for the flag
Optional: 1 yd. of coordinating fabric for
    square napkins (16" finished size)

Cutting Directions

From novelty flag fabric, cut:

• four 13¼" x 14" pieces

From the backing fabric, cut away selvage
edges only. Do not cut this into four pieces.

From the white fabric, cut:

• four 7¼" x 14" pieces

From the red fabric, cut:

• eight 1⅜" strips for the single-layer
    binding

• 7" x 18" rectangle for the red flag stripes

From the 7" square of navy blue fabric, cut

• 4 shapes using the template on page
    121 (Cut navy fabric AFTER attaching
    paper-backed fusible web.)

Hint

When cutting the novelty
flag fabric, keep in mind that
the 14" side is sewn to the
white fabric. Make sure to cut
directional fabrics accordingly.

Optional: Cut the napkin fabric into four
equal 18" squares.

1 Trace four star sections found on page 121 onto the 6½" square of fusible web for the stars of the flag. Trace 12 long red stripes and 16 short red stripes onto the 6½" x 17" piece of fusible web for the red stripes of the flag. Stripe patterns are found on page 121.

2 Following the manufacturer's directions, fuse the 6½" square of fusible web to the wrong side of the 7" square of navy blue fabric. Fuse the 6½" x 17" fusible web to the wrong side of the 7" x 18" red fabric rectangle.

3 Cut out each piece. Each place mat will use one star section, four short red stripes, and three long red stripes.

4 Arrange the pieces of the flag on each of the 7¼" x 14" pieces of white fabric as illustrated. After removing the paper backing, arrange the pieces of the flag on the white background.

5 Tuck the left edges of the short red stripes under the star fabric. Fuse all pieces to the background according to the directions that accompany the fusible web.

6 Thread your machine with coordinating red thread. Using a reduced-size blanket stitch, or a reduced-size zigzag stitch, sew around each stripe. Do not sew the sides of the short red stripes which are underneath the star fabric. When the stripes are finished on all four place mats, change the thread to navy blue. Using a reduced-size blanket stitch, or a reduced-size zigzag stitch, sew around each star section.

7 With right sides together, attach one white section to one novelty print section, making sure that any directional fabric is facing the same direction as the flag. Sew these 14" long seams using a ¼" seam allowance. Press the seam towards the white fabric.

8 Using a contrasting marker, mark your straight lines on the novelty print. The quilting lines of the sample are spaced 1" apart.

4

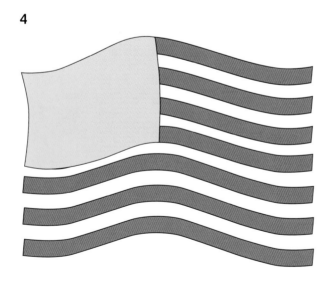

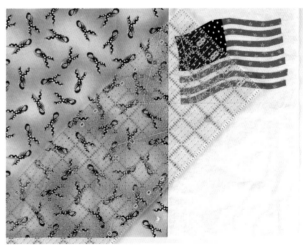

Using the 45-degree line on the ruler, mark your lines on the novelty print fabric in preparation for the straight-line quilting.

9 Following the directions starting on page 23, secure the entire piece of backing fabric to your table. Smooth the batting over the backing. Finally, evenly space each place-mat top over the batting. Pin baste. When the basting is complete, separate the four place mats by cutting through the batting and backing. Then remove the masking tape.

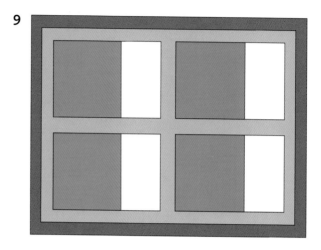

10 Straight-line quilt the novelty print area. Quilt the white section using random meandering. Stitch around the flag.

The back of the place mat shows the quilting patterns. The quilting between the red stripes makes them puff out. Stitch-in-the-ditch was used in the seam to get from one straight line to the next in the center of the quilt.

11 When the quilting is complete, cut away the excess backing and batting. Bind the place mats following the directions on page 117.

12 OPTIONAL: To complete the napkins, press over each raw edge to the back ¼" around all four sides. Secure each raw edge to the back using a reduced-size zigzag stitch to eliminate fraying.

Table Toppers

This Table Topper will help you:

- See how different quilting patterns change a quilt top.
- Use a quilting pattern that emanates from the center out.

Hint

Because of the way the 22½-degree ruler cuts the wedges, you end up with two quilt tops. Try quilting one top with a straight-line pattern and the other with a free-motion pattern.

Finished size: 23" diameter before quilting

Materials

Sewing machine and accessories from
   page 81
Neutral thread used for piecing
Quilting thread
22½-degree rotary cutting ruler by
   Nifty Notions
7" square of freezer paper
Two 6" squares of iron-on/tear-away
   stabilizer
40" x 48" piece of batting
Polyester monofilament thread

Fabric

Five fat quarters
8" square of fabric for the center circles
One fat quarter for the binding
1⅓ yd. of fabric for the backing fabric

> ### Hint
> The samples were constructed
> using batik fabrics, but any
> fabric can be used.

Cutting Directions

From each of the five fat quarters, cut:

• six 2½" x 21" strips

From the fat quarter for the binding, cut:

• eight 1⅜" wide strips

> ### Hint
> Cut all strips on the cross-grain
> of the fabric.

1 Arrange your fabric strips in the order you want to piece them. Sew six sets of strip sets.

1

> ### Hint
> Be sure to sew all of the fabrics in all
> of the strip sets in the same order.

2 Press all of the seams of three strip sets up, and press all of the seams of three strip sets down. Paying careful attention to the pressing details now will make piecing the wedges easier.

3 Use the 22½-degree wedge ruler to cut only one strip set at a time. Place the 8¼" line of the wedge tool directly over the top seam of the first strip set. Cut on both sides of the wedge tool.

3

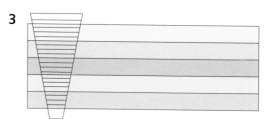

By placing the 8¼" line over a seam, the wedges will be cut accurately.

4

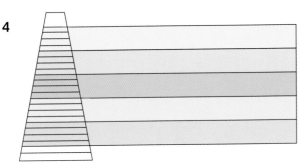

Make sure to line the left side of the ruler up to the first cut.

4 Flip the ruler upside down and place the 8¼" line directly over the bottom seam, and cut another wedge.

5 Continue to cut the remaining strip sets. Flip the ruler right side up, then upside down until the first strip set is cut. Repeat Steps 3 through 5 on the remaining five strip sets.

6

Keep these piles organized!

a.   b.

c.   d.

6 Organize your wedges into four piles:
   a. The first pile is comprised of eight wedges with the first color on the top edge, and the seams pressed down.
   b. The second pile is comprised of eight wedges with the first color on the top edge, and the seams pressed up.
   c. The third pile is comprised of eight wedges with the fifth color on the top edge, and the seams pressed down.
   d. The fourth pile is comprised of eight wedges with the fifth color on the top edge, and the seams pressed up.

7

Double check to make sure that the seams are pressed in alternating directions all the way around.

7 Set the third and fourth piles aside and work only on the first and second piles. Arrange the wedges in a circular pattern alternating the wedges according to the way the seams are pressed.

8 Sew the sixteen wedges together. Do not press any seams until all the wedges have been pieced. When the wedges have been pieced into a circle, press the seams open to reduce bulk at the seams.

9 Press one of the iron-on/tear-away stabilizer sheets to the wrong side of the table topper, directly over the hole. Set the quilt top aside temporarily.

10 Fold the freezer paper in half with shiny sides together. Trace a 2¾" diameter circle onto one side of the freezer paper using the template on page 121. Cut out two circles. Press both circles to the wrong side of the 8" square of fabric for the center circles. Place the circles far enough apart on the 8" square so that there is ample seam allowance around both circles. Cut out each circle, leaving at least ¼" of fabric beyond the freezer paper for your seam allowance.

11 Fold the seam allowance to the back, and hand baste the seam allowance to the freezer paper in the back of the circles. Set one circle aside for the second table topper.

12 Thread the sewing machine with the monofilament thread. Set up your sewing machine for a narrow blind-hem stitch or a narrow zigzag stitch. Center your circle to the middle of the table topper. Pin the circle to the right side of the table topper, inserting the pins into the stabilizer. Sew the circle to the table topper.

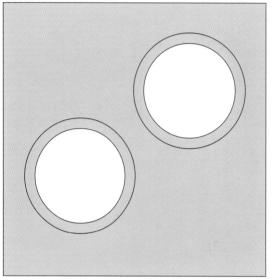

10

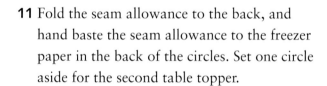

While each table topper uses only one center circle, it saves time to complete both circles now.

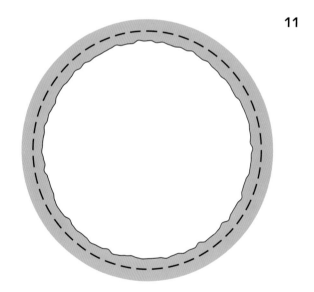

11

The freezer paper helps you to form a perfectly round circle.

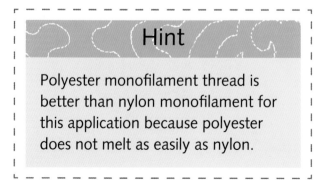

Hint

Polyester monofilament thread is better than nylon monofilament for this application because polyester does not melt as easily as nylon.

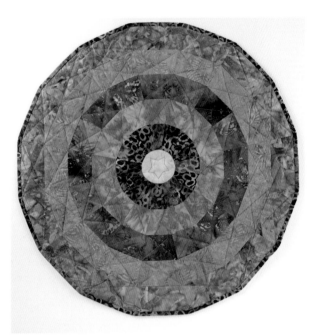

This is what it looks like from the front.

13 Tear away the stabilizer from the wrong side. Remove your basting stitches from the center circle, and then pull out the freezer paper. Starting at Step 8, piece the second table topper.

Pin baste the backing, batting and backing following the directions on page 23. The batting and backing yardage is sufficient to pin baste both table toppers at one time to large backing and batting pieces. See page 97 to see an example of the Americana Place Mats pin basted at one time.

One of the sample table toppers was completed using several unmarked free-motion quilting patterns. The other was quilted using continuous straight-line quilting. On the straight-line example, I started at the outside raw edge. I stitched diagonal lines through each "square," stopping to pivot at each seam intersection. A star was marked in the center circle, and stitched with contrasting thread.

After you have finished the quilting, bind each table topper using the instructions found on page 117.

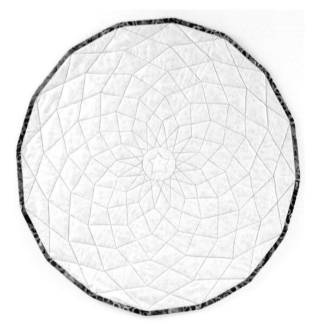

This is the straight-line quilting example from the back. It is a lovely finish.

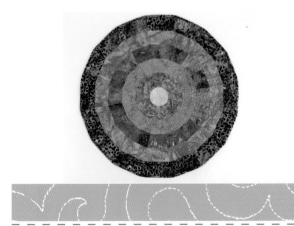

Autumn Nights

This large wall hanging will help you:

• Learn to stabilize and smooth over intricate piecing with free-motion quilting.

• Practice quilting points and stars.

• Get used to a larger-sized project. After you quilt this project, a twin-size quilt is your next step!

Hint: Before beginning each star, gather all cut fabrics for that star,
so the cut fabrics don't get mixed together.

Finished size: 48" x 48" before quilting

Materials

Sewing machine and accessories from
    page 81
Neutral thread used for piecing
Quilting thread
Rotary cutter and mat
6" x 24" ruler for cutting strips
4" square-up ruler
12½" square-up ruler

Cutting Directions

From the seasonal border print, cut:
- Five 5½" strips. Set these strips aside for
  the borders.
- One 2½" strip. From this strip, cut four
  2½" x 4½" rectangles. Set these aside for
  1st star.
- One 2" strip. Set this strip aside for 3rd star.
- Six 1⅜" strips. Set aside for binding.

From the background print, cut:
- Two 2½" strips. From these strips cut
  12 2½" squares and four 2½" x 4½"
  rectangles. Set these aside for star #1.
- Three 2¾" strips. From these strips cut
  16 2¾" x 5" rectangles and sixteen 2¾"
  squares. Set these aside for star #2.
- One 2" strip. Set this strip aside for star #3.
- One 3½" strip. From this strip cut 16
  3½" x 2" rectangles. Set these aside for
  star #3.
- One 4¼" strip. From this strip cut four 4¼"
  squares. Set these aside for star #3.
- Two 4" strips. From these strips cut four
  10½" x 4" rectangles, and four 8½" x 4"
  rectangles. Set these aside for the 4th star.

Fabric

1¼ yd. of a seasonal autumn print for the
    borders, binding, and two of the stars
1¼ yd. for the background (gold)
½ yd. of dark A (plaid)
⅓ yd. of dark B (green)
⅜ yd. of dark C (red)
⅜ yd. of dark D (green) for the inner
    border and small stars
3 yd. of backing fabric (there will be
    some unused fabric)

- Three 1½" strips. From these strips cut eight
  9½" x 1½" lengths, and four 10½" x 1½"
  lengths. Set these aside for the filler strips.
- Two 2½" strips. From these strips cut four
  12½" x 2½" pieces, four 2½" squares, and
  four 2" x 2½" pieces. Set these aside for the
  4th star.

From the dark A fabric (orange and green plaid)
cut:
- One 2½" strip. From this strip cut four
  6½" x 2½" rectangles. Set these aside for star
  #1.
- Three 2¾" strips. From these strips cut 32
  2¾" squares. Set these aside for star #2.
- One 4¼" strip. From this strip cut four 4¼"
  squares. Set these aside for star #3.

From the dark B fabric (green) cut:
- One 2½" strip. From this strip cut four 2½"
  squares. Set these aside for star #1.
- One 7" x 14" panel. Set this aside for star #2.
- One 4¼" strip. From this strip cut four 4¼"
  squares. Set these aside for star #3.

From the dark C fabric (red) cut:

Cutting Directions (continued)

- One 7" x 14" panel. Set this aside for star #2.
- One 4¼" strip. From this strip cut eight 4¼" squares. Set these aside for star #3.

From the dark D fabric cut:

- Four 1½" strips. Set these aside for the inner border.
- Two 2½" strips. From these strips cut 20 2½" squares. Set these aside for star #4.

Hint

Cut all strips on the cross-grain of the fabric.

This wall hanging has a series of nine-patch blocks. No matter what size the blocks are, the piecing is identical. The basic directions for sewing a nine-patch block are as follows.

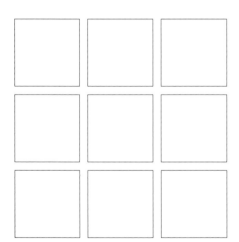

Step 1 *Arrange the nine pieces to be included in the block.*

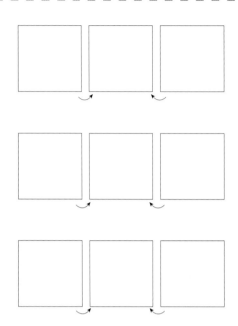

Step 2 *Sew together the three blocks in each row.*

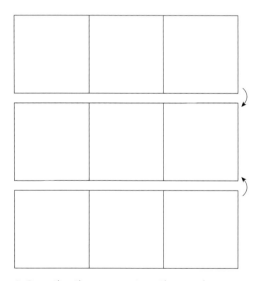

Step 3 *Sew the three rows together and press up.*

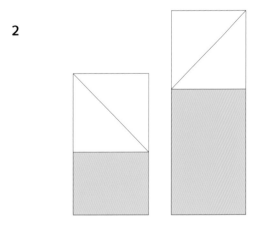

The quilt has only one 12" square star.

Making the Center Star (Star #1)

Unless sewing directly on a marked line, all seams are sewn using a ¼" seam allowance.

1 Take eight of the 2½" background squares and mark a diagonal line on the wrong side of each square. Mark the line from one corner to its opposite corner.

2 With right sides together, place one square at one end of each of the 6½" x 2½" rectangles, and one square at one end of each of the 4½" x 2½" rectangles as shown. The diagonal line on the square being attached to the short rectangle goes from the top left corner to the bottom right corner. The diagonal line on the square being attached to the larger rectangle goes from bottom left corner to the top right corner. Sew along the marked diagonal line for all eight pieces.

3 Placing the ¼" line of your square-up ruler directly over the sewing line, cut away the excess fabric. On the 6½" pieces, press towards the triangle. On the 4½" pieces, press towards the rectangle.

1

2

Notice how the diagonal lines of the background squares are arranged on the rectangles going in opposite directions.

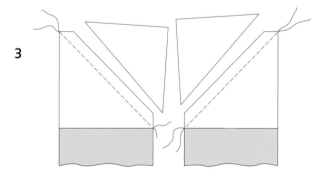

Be sure to use a dry iron when pressing these pieces.

4 Take the remaining four 2½" background squares, and piece one of them to each of the 2½" dark fabric B (green) squares. Press to the green square. To each of these, attach one 2½" x 4½" background piece. Press to the background fabric.

5 Sew the pieced 2½" x 4½" rectangle to one of the 4½" squares as shown. Press to the 4½" square. Then attach one 6½" x 2½" section as shown. Press to the 6½" strip. Repeat this step for the remaining three sections.

6 Sew the four 6½" squares together as shown. Pieced, this star should measure approximately 12½" square.

Making the Second Star

The quilt requires four of these 9" finished-sized stars.

4

Pieced, this square should measure 4½" square.

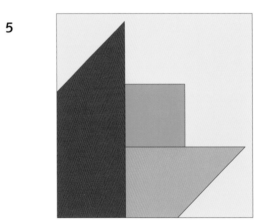

5

You will have four of these.

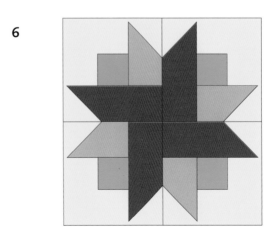

6

After pressing, set this star aside.

7 **8**

After sewing, the horizontal, vertical, and diagonal lines will be cutting lines, so accurate marking is important.

11

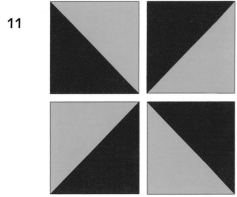

Press the last seam on the back open to minimize bulk in the center.

12

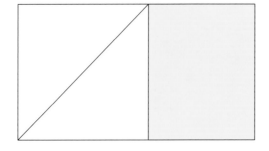

Since you are forming the star points here, it is important to make sure the diagonal line is facing the correct direction.

7 Using the two 7" x 14" fabric B and fabric C panels, determine which one is the lightest on the wrong side. On the wrong side of the lightest fabric, mark a grid, dividing the panel into eight equal-sized squares. The three vertical lines are 3½" apart, and the single horizontal line is marked through the center. Next, mark diagonal lines in only one direction as shown. With right sides together, place the marked panel over the unmarked panel.

8 Sew a ¼" seam on both sides of the diagonal lines. Press flat after sewing.

9 Cut apart the half triangle squares at the vertical, horizontal and diagonal lines. Press the half-triangle squares open towards the red side. You should have a total of 16 half-triangle squares.

10 Square up all 16 of the half-triangle squares to 2¾" square. While "squaring up" is often an inconvenient step, the results are worth the effort.

11 Arrange four half-triangle squares into pinwheel formations. Sew the top two squares together and press to the green. Sew the bottom two squares together, and press to the green. Finally, sew the two rectangles together, and press the seams open. Make four of these.

12 Mark a diagonal line on the wrong side of each of the thirty-two dark fabric A 2¾" squares (see Step 1 illustration). Set 16 marked squares to the side. Arrange one fabric A square at one end of each of the 16 5" x 2¾" background rectangles, and sew on the marked line.

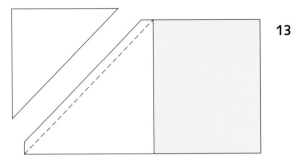

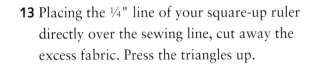

13 Placing the ¼" line of your square-up ruler directly over the sewing line, cut away the excess fabric. Press the triangles up.

Do not use steam when pressing the triangles up.

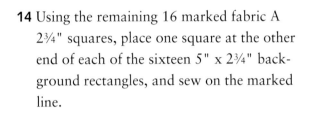

14 Using the remaining 16 marked fabric A 2¾" squares, place one square at the other end of each of the sixteen 5" x 2¾" background rectangles, and sew on the marked line.

15 Placing the ¼" line of your square-up ruler directly over the sewing line, cut away the excess fabric. Press the triangles up.

The points for this star are formed from making these "flying geese" rectangles.

16 Using four 2¾" background squares, four flying geese, and one pin wheel, arrange these nine parts to prepare sewing them together as a typical nine-patch block.

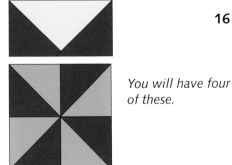

You will have four of these.

17 Sew these nine pieces together following the directions on page 105 for piecing together a nine-patch block. Repeat this step for the remaining three #2 stars.

The quilt requires four of these 9" finished-sized stars. This star is the same outside shape of the center star, however, it is pieced using quarter-square triangles.

Making the Third Star

18 Take all twenty of the 4¼" squares that were set aside for the 3rd star, and cut them into quarters using diagonal cuts as shown.

19 After all twenty squares have been cut, organize the triangles into four color groups. You will have four background triangles, eight fabric C triangles, four fabric A triangles, and four fabric B triangles.

20 Begin to piece all of the quarter-square triangles into five separate squares as shown.

Hint

Arrange the triangles for all four of these stars on your cutting table. If you are worried about making an error, simply piece one star at a time.

18

For the sake of accuracy, do not cut more than two or three layers of squares at a time.

20  *Make eight of these squares.*

  Make eight of these squares.

  Make four of these squares.

21 Check to make sure that each pieced square measures 3½". Before moving on to the next step, clip away the points sticking out around the edges.

22

From the pieced strips, cut 16 2" sections.

22 Sew the long 2" border-fabric strip to the long, 2" background-fabric strip. Press to the border print. After squaring up one end, cut away 16 2" sections.

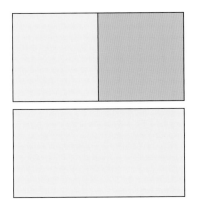

23

You will use four of these completed squares in each star.

23 To each of the sections you cut in step 22, attach one 2" x 3½" background piece. Press to the background fabric.

24 The final piecing of the 3rd star can now be completed. Arrange the four stars as shown. (Y stands for background fabric.)

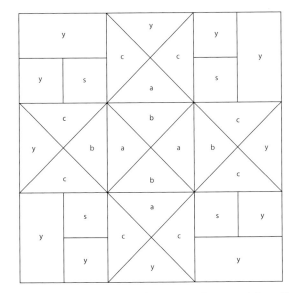

24

Notice that the dark fabric C (red) is used for all of the star points. Dark colors A and B are alternately arranged in the center to create interest.

25 Sew these nine pieces together following the directions on page 105 on piecing together a nine-patch block. Repeat this step for the remaining three #3 stars.

The quilt requires four of these 6" stars. This star is the easiest to complete because it is pieced automatically when the background filler strips are connected.

Making the Fourth Star and Background Filler Sections

26 Using 16 of the 2½" fabric D squares, mark a diagonal line on the back of each square. Mark the line from one corner to its opposite corner. (See the illustration at Step 1.)

27 Using eight of the marked 2½" squares from Step 26, and the four 12½" x 2½" background filler strips, place one marked 2½" square on each end of the filler strips as shown. It is important that the diagonal lines on BOTH ends extend from the lower left corner to the upper right corner. Then sew on the marked line. Cut away the excess fabric, and press the triangles out.

27

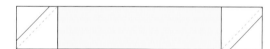

While the diagonal lines must face in the same direction for sewing, when opened, the triangles will point in opposite directions.

28

Press the squares out.

28 Take the four unmarked 2½" fabric D squares, attach one square to each end of two of the pieced strips from Step 27.

29

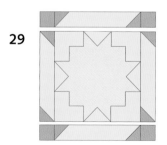

29 Arrange the strips from Steps 26 and 27 around the 12" center star as shown. Pieced, it should measure approximately 16½" square. When completed, set aside.

Join the short strips to each side of the center star, then add the remaining pieced strips from step 27 to the top and bottom as illustrated.

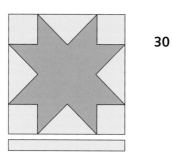

30

Since the #2 stars are non-directional, the filler strip can be attached to any edge.

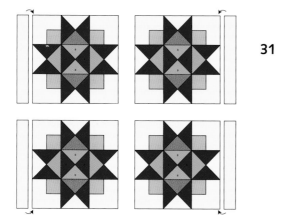

31

Because these stars are directional, each filler strip needs to be attached to a different side of all four stars. Use the center square to maintain your orientation.

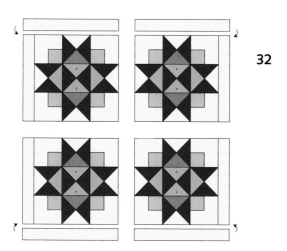

32

Because these stars are directional, the second filler strip needs to be added as illustrated. Use the center square to maintain your orientation.

30 Take the four #2 stars and attach one of the 1½" x 9½" background filler strips to the bottom of each #2 star. Press to the background.

31 Take the four #3 stars and attach one of the remaining 1½" x 9½" background filler strips to one of the sides of each #3 star.

32 Add the 1½" x 10½" background filler strips to one of the sides of each #3 star.

33 Take the four remaining marked 2½" fabric D squares, and the four 2½" background squares that were cut and set aside for the #4 stars. With right sides together, sew one of the fabric D squares to one of the background squares. Sew along the diagonal line. Then trim away the excess fabric and press the seam towards the fabric D triangle.

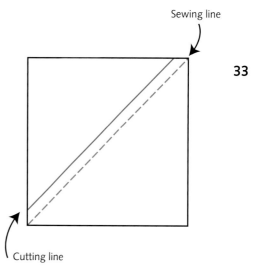

33

Repeat this three more times to the remaining squares.

34

Make sure you are joining the 2" x 2½" background piece to the colored triangle, with the point facing down.

34 Attach one 2" x 2½" piece to each one of the half-triangle squares from Step 33. After the piecing is completed, the piece should measure 2½" x 4". You need four of these.

35

The finished size of these rectangles is 10½" x 4".

35 Each of the four 2½" x 4" pieced sections from the previous step now need to be sewn to one of the 8½" x 4" background sections as shown.

36

Sew along the diagonal line marked in blue. Cut away the excess fabric ¼" from the seam as shown in red. Press the triangle up.

36 Find each of the 10½" x 4" background sections, and the four remaining 2½" marked fabric D squares. Place one square on each one of the large background panels as illustrated. Stitch through the marked diagonal line. Cut away the excess fabric, then press the triangle up.

37

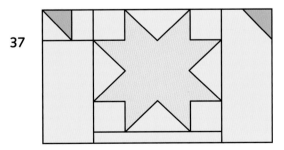

You'll have four #2 stars with one of each pieced background panels. They should measure approximately 16½" x 10½".

37 Arrange the four #2 stars, and the pieced background panels from Steps 34 and 35 as shown. Sew these border panels to each side of the #2 stars, then press the seams to the background.

38 It is finally time to piece the center of this wall hanging. Arrange the nine blocks as shown.

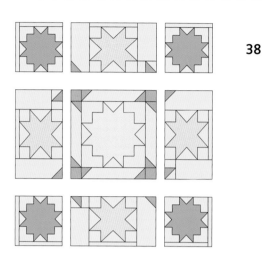

You can really start to see the 4th star taking shape.

39 Sew these nine pieces together following the directions on page 105 on piecing together a nine-patch block. The only difference is that this is a very large nine-patch block.

40 It is time, now, to add the inner border. Measure the width of the quilt top across the center. Then cut two of the 1½" inner border strips to that length. Sew one strip to the top, and one strip to the bottom of the quilt top. Press the strips out carefully.

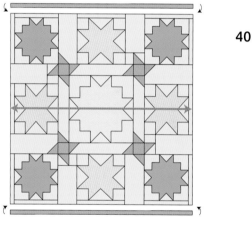

40

Measure the width at the center

41 Measure the length of the quilt top down the center. Then trim the remaining two 1½" inner border strips to that length. Sew one strip to each side. Press the strips out carefully.

42 The outer border is attached the same way the inner border was attached. Since the border strips are not long enough on two sides, two of the border strips need to be pieced. Cut away the selvage edges on all five border strips. Cut one of the 5½" border strips in half at the fold of the fabric. Attach each of the short lengths to two of the longer strips. Press the seams toward the long strip. Set these two strips aside for Step 44.

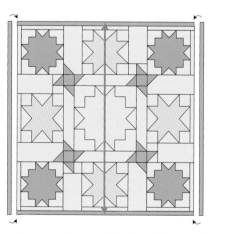

41

Measure the length down the center

43

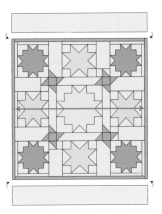

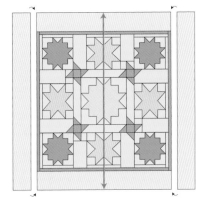

Measure the width at the center.

44

43 Measure the width of the quilt top across the center. Then cut the two remaining 5½" outer-border strips to that length. Sew one strip to the top, and one strip to the bottom of the quilt top. Press the strips out.

44 Measure the length of the quilt top down the center. Then trim the remaining two 5½" outer-border strips to that length. Sew one strip to each side. Press the strips out.

45 The backing is pieced from two 54" lengths of fabric. Cut off all selvage edges, then with right sides together, join the two 54" x 40" panels along the 54" length. Trim this 54" x 79" panel to a 54" square to use as the backing piece.

Measure the length down the center.

All the piecing is completed. Pin baste the backing, batting, and quilt top according to the directions starting on page 26.

Each of the stars of the sample was quilted using four different unmarked free-motion quilting patterns. Star #4 used a copper-colored metallic thread. The background was quilted using a medium-size random meandering pattern with 100% hand-dyed cotton thread. The inner border was quilted using gentle wavy lines, and stitch-in-the-ditch at the seam where the outer border is joined to the inner border. Finally, the outer border was quilted with a variety of leaves to mimic the autumn leaves in the fabric.

For quilting ideas, see the close-up photographs of each star. A sample of the border quilting appears on page 64. The background was quilted using a medium-size random-meandering pattern. The inner border was quilted using gentle wavy lines and stitch-in-the-ditch at the seam between the inner and outer borders.

After the quilting is completed, cut away the excess batting and backing. Follow the binding instructions on page 117.

Binding

Like all quilting, binding is a personal preference. Many quilt instructions use 2½" wide strips pressed in half for the binding. This means that there are six layers of binding fabric, one layer of backing, one layer of batting, and the quilt top all the way around the edge of the quilt. After using this technique on a few projects, I found that the weight of the fabric could adversely affect the drape of the completed quilt. In fact, on a small project, it is a lot like putting a straight-jacket on a quilt. Therefore, I now use only a single-layer technique. It takes a bit longer to feed the binding through the bias tape maker, but I am always rewarded with gracefully hanging quilts. The yardage allowances in all of the projects for this book use this single-layer technique. Should you wish to use the pressed-in-half, 2½" binding strips, alter the yardage requirements accordingly.

Materials

Sewing machine and accessories from page 81

Neutral thread used for piecing

Size 18 Clover Bias Tape Maker

1 Cut enough 1⅜" wide binding strips to go all the way around your quilt, plus an additional 12" to 15". The additional length provides enough binding to make the mitered corners and to join the beginning and ending binding tails.

2 Connect the binding strips together with a diagonal seam. After sewing, trim the excess away.

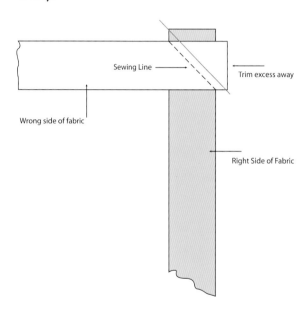

Sewing Line

Trim excess away

Wrong side of fabric

Right Side of Fabric

3 Press each seam open. Use a dry iron for this step.

4 Feed one end of the binding into the bias tape maker, following the directions of the manufacturer. Press the binding as it comes out of the bias tape maker. Be careful not to stretch the fabric as you pull it through the bias tape maker.

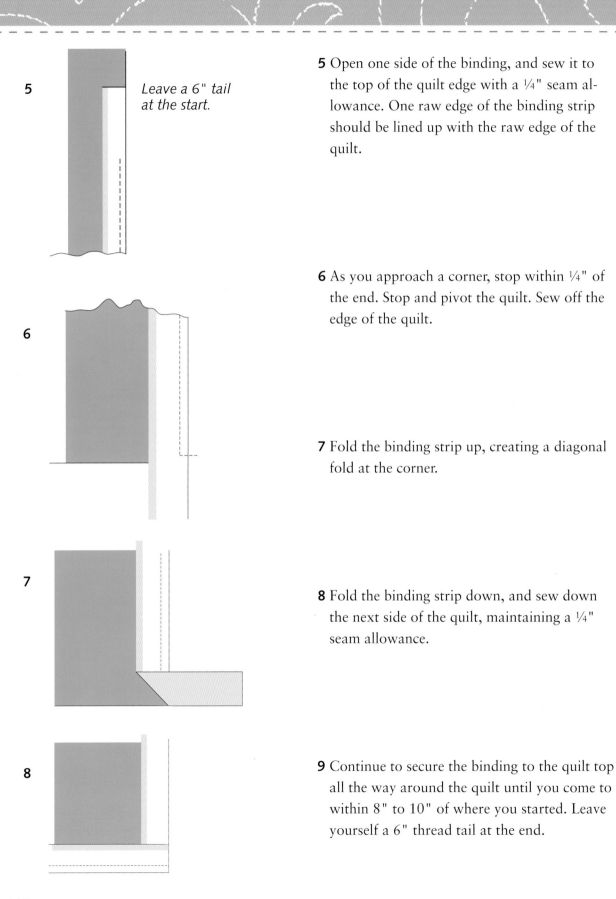

5 Leave a 6" tail at the start.

5 Open one side of the binding, and sew it to the top of the quilt edge with a ¼" seam allowance. One raw edge of the binding strip should be lined up with the raw edge of the quilt.

6 As you approach a corner, stop within ¼" of the end. Stop and pivot the quilt. Sew off the edge of the quilt.

6

7 Fold the binding strip up, creating a diagonal fold at the corner.

7

8 Fold the binding strip down, and sew down the next side of the quilt, maintaining a ¼" seam allowance.

8

9 Continue to secure the binding to the quilt top all the way around the quilt until you come to within 8" to 10" of where you started. Leave yourself a 6" thread tail at the end.

10 Open the binding tails. Fold the ending tail up creating a diagonal fold. Fold the starting tail down, forming a diagonal fold. Adjust the diagonal folds until the binding tails meet in the center. Finger press.

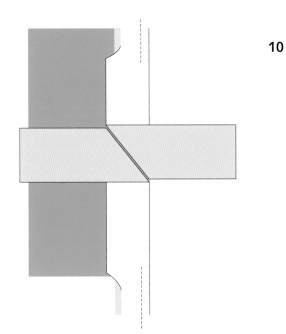

10

11 Pin the binding tails together where the diagonal folds meet. Sew the binding tails together following the diagonal line. Trim away the excess binding fabric, and finger press the seam open.

12 Stitch the remaining binding section to the quilt.

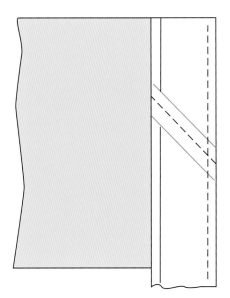

11

13 Fold the binding to the back of the quilt. Maintaining the folded edge of the binding, hand-stitch the binding to the back of the quilt. Miter the binding at the corners and hand stitch in place.

Don't forget to add your label to the back of the quilt!

Templates

Sweet Hearts (page 91)

1st heart
Trace 1

5th heart
Trace 2

2nd heart
Trace 1

3rd heart
Trace 3

4th heart
Trace 2

7th heart
Trace 4

6th heart
Trace 3

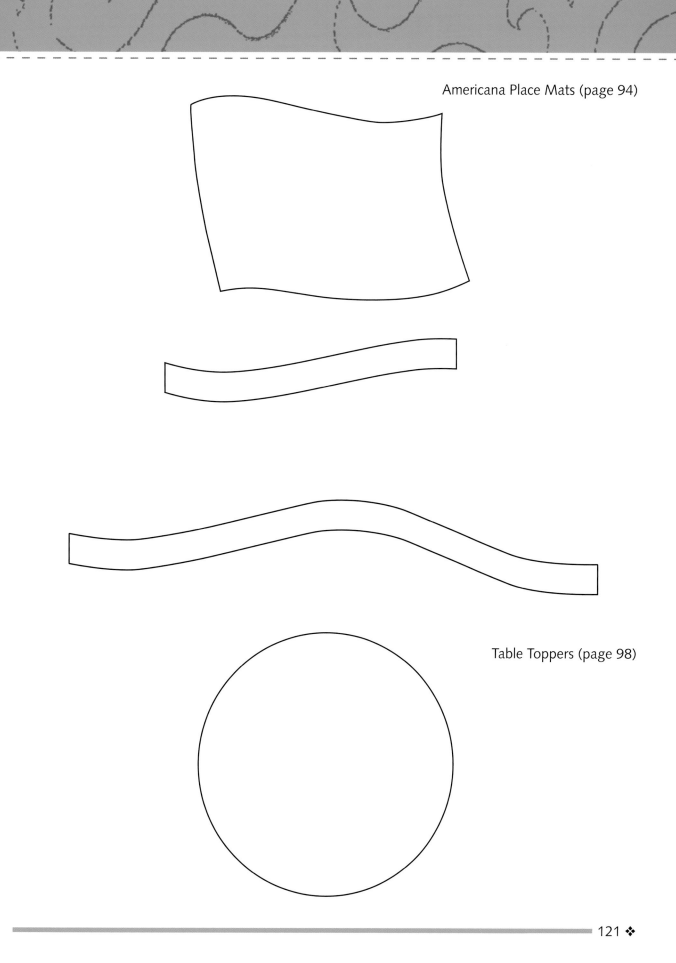

Americana Place Mats (page 94)

Table Toppers (page 98)

Practice Patterns

Photocopy the pattern you'd like to practice. Remove the thread from your machine and stitch the paper following the lines. Remember to use good quilting posture. Do not rotate the sheet of paper as you move it across the machine bed. Notice how often you are changing directions. You are developing muscle memory as you move the piece of paper under the machine. After practicing several times, you will be able to quilt the pattern from memory! Even after you've mastered a pattern, it's a good idea to practice a pattern as a warm up, especially if you haven't quilted that pattern in a while.

Random Meandering
(page 56)

Loops (page 58)

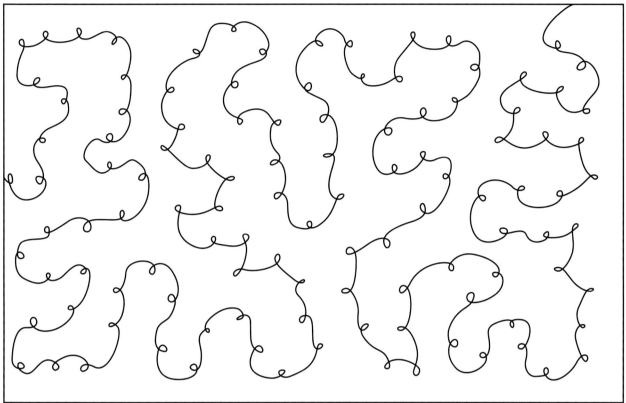

Flames (page 59)

Landscape Texture (page 60)

Swirls and Curls (page 61)

Try-Angles (page 62)

About the Author

Charlene Frable is a professional educator by trade, and a quilt teacher by choice.

Charlene has over 40 years of sewing experience. She first learned to sew when her mother sent her to the home of a neighbor who was a home economics teacher. Charlene also attended their local YWCA for summer classes. Eventually she became proficient at sewing her own garments and home décor projects. Her passion for sewing took a sudden turn towards quilting in 1992.

All of Charlene's quilts are machine quilted using one of her domestic sewing machines. She feels that every quilt makes her a better quilter. And the amazing variety of domestic and imported threads, along with an endless supply of commercial fabrics, have made quilting a dynamic, living art form.

For the last ten years she has been teaching domestic sewing machine quilting classes. Her sense of humor and practical approach have made her technique classes popular amongst novice quilters. Charlene also teaches classes based on original quilt designs.

Charlene feels that teaching is a great learning experience. When she taught her first free-motion class, she was as nervous as the participants, but they persevered and had a great time.

Her favorite part of teaching is getting to know other quilters. She enjoys the stories from quilters, how they got started in quilting, what inspires them, and who the lucky recipients of their quilts will be. She loves the versatility of quilting because no matter what a quilter's skill level, everyone can be successful.

Charlene and her husband, Barry, live in Lehighton, Pennsylvania with their dogs, Banjo and Holly.

Resources

Allentown Sewing Machine Outlet
725 N. 15th Street, Rear
Allentown, PA 18102
800-797-0124
www.allentownsewing.com

Annie's Attic
1 Annie Lane
Big Sandy, TX 75755
Phone: 800-582-6643
www.anniesattic.com

Clotilde, LLC
P.O. Box 7500
Big Sandy, TX 75755-7500
Phone: 800-772-2891
www.clotilde.com

Connecting Threads
P.O. Box 870760
Vancouver, WA 98687-7760
Phone: 800-574-6454
www.ConnectingThreads.com

Ghee's
2620 Centenary Blvd. No. 2-250
Shreveport, LA 71104
Phone: 318-226-1701
E-mail: bags@ghees.com
www.ghees.com

Herrschners, Inc.
2800 Hoover Road
Stevens Point, WI 54492-0001
Phone: 800-441-0838
www.herrschners.com/

Home Sew
P.O. Box 4099
Bethlehem, PA 18018-0099
Phone: 800-344-4739
www.homesew.com

Keepsake Quilting
Route 25
P.O. Box 1618
Center Harbor, NH 03226-1618
Phone: 800-438-5464
www.keepsakequilting.com

Krause Publications
700 E. State St.
Iola, WI 54990
Phone: 800-258-0929
www.krausebooks.com

Nancy's Notions
333 Beichl Ave.
P.O. Box 683
Beaver Dam, WI 53916-0683
Phone: 800-833-0690
www.nancysnotions.com

Tacony Corporation
1760 Gilsinn Lane
Fenton, MO 63026
800-313-4110
www.tacony.com

Web of Thread
18208 66th Ave NE, Suite 102
Kenmore, WA 98028
800-955-8185
www.webofthread.com

Books I Can't Live Without
See ordering information on next page.

For a thorough review of precision piecing techniques and tips:

Everyone Can Quilt with Kay Wood
by Kay Wood

For a detailed discussion of machine quilting using stencils with tracing paper:

Elegant Machine Quilting
by Joanie Zeier Poole

For fresh ideas on binding and borders:

The Quilter's Edge
by Darlene Zimmerman

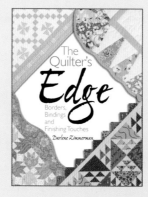